WITNESS TO WAR

The Civil War: 1861–1865

THE CIVIL WAR: 1861–1865

Harold Holzer

A PERIGEE BOOK

A Perigee Book
Published by The Berkley Publishing Group
200 Madison Avenue
New York, NY 10016

First edition: May 1996

Published simultaneously in Canada.

The Putnam Berkley World Wide Web site address is
http://www.berkley.com

Library of Congress Cataloging-in-Publication Data

Holzer, Harold.
    Witness to War : the Civil War, 1861–1865 / Harold Holzer. —
1st ed.
        p.   cm.
    ISBN 0-399-52203-4
    1. United States—History—Civil War, 1861–1865—
Anecdotes.   2. United States—History—Civil War, 1861–
1865—Quotations, maxims, etc.   I. Title.
E655.H75   1996   95-25949
973.7—dc20   CIP

Printed in the United States of America

10   9   8   7   6   5   4   3   2   1

CONTENTS

ACKNOWLEDGMENTS

To assemble this collection, I turned not only to the vast literature of the Civil War, but to the generous fraternity of Civil War scholars, many among them my good friends. They shared with me their favorite quotations and passages, patiently answered my letters, freely offered recommendations and admonitions, and in some cases even gave permission to use material they had uncovered for their own works-in-progress. I am most grateful to them all.

I must thank particularly John Y. Simon, editor of *The Papers of Ulysses S. Grant,* who led me to a number of wonderful, seldom-quoted lines by the Union commander. I thank, too, James M. McPherson of Princeton University, who offered some remarkable letters he uncovered for his forthcoming study, *Why They Fought.* Mark E. Neely, Jr., of St. Louis University, convincingly shared with me his enthusiasm for the still-undervalued writings of William T. Sherman. George M. Craig, President of the Civil War Round Table of New York, made crucial and most useful suggestions about his hero, Gen. George H. Thomas. And Frank J. Williams, longtime president of the Abraham Lincoln Association, cheerfully and indispensably, as always, made available the resources of his peerless library and collection, and burned the midnight fax machine to respond to my frequent requests with unfailing speed.

Lauren Cook Burgess and the Minerva Center of Pasadena, California, agreed to allow me to excerpt quotations from *An Uncommon Soldier*, and Walbrook Swank and White Main Publishing of Shippensburg, Pennsylvania, granted permission to consult and use material from *Confederate Letters and Diaries, 1861–1865*. I thank these editors and publishers, too, for their thoughtfulness.

Above all, I am grateful to John Duff, my former editor at Doubleday, now the publisher of Perigee Books, who first came to me and asked me to compile this collection. It is always gratifying when old colleagues renew happy associations, particularly when they offer projects as rewarding as this one proved to be for me.

Finally, my family provided its usual, crucial dose of support and patience. My wife, Edith, and my daughters, Remy and Meg, are never at a loss for words—particularly words of encouragement—and these proved particularly valuable when my own search for words from the past was yielding few gems. Happily, the search ultimately led to innumerable treasures, thanks in large measure to the people I have cited.

Inevitably, however, any such book excludes more material than an editor would like, and this compilation is no exception. All of the colleagues named above are entitled to share with me the credit for the extraordinary words this volume resurrects; but, needless to say, the responsibility for any and all omissions are mine alone.

—Harold Holzer
Rye, New York
April 1, 1995

INTRODUCTION: THE "INCOMMUNICABLE EXPERIENCE OF WAR"

ON A MEMORIAL DAY nearly twenty years after the last gun had maimed the last victim of the American Civil War, a onetime Union captain—and future Supreme Court justice—stood before his fellow veterans and spoke with unexpected longing of what he insisted was the "great good fortune" of their common history.

"In our youths," he explained, "our hearts were touched with fire."

To the speaker on that day, Oliver Wendell Holmes, Jr., nothing he had accomplished since—neither his work as a Harvard law professor nor his service as a Massachusetts jurist—had ever rekindled "the passion of life to its top" that he had felt at Ball's Bluff, Antietam, Fredericksburg, and other blood-soaked battle-fields of the Civil War.

What was it that had proven so wrenching, yet so vivid and heady, that the experience remained indelible, even central, to a man who had come so far since? What was it about those times that made a famous man of peace so nostalgic about the horrors of war?

Even the eloquent Holmes could not quite find the words to explain. All he could do on that Memorial Day twenty years later was remind his fellow survivors: "We have shared the incommunicable experience of war."

In truth they had shared—and communicated—a great deal more. As an aging civilian, Holmes may have regarded his dim wartime memories as "incommunicable," but as a youthful officer he had ably reported what he was living through, both in a revealing personal diary and in haunting letters to his father, a famous writer. Those experiences, he once wrote home from the front lines, had transformed him practically overnight from boy to man.

It has been said that the Civil War transformed the entire *country* from adolescence to maturity. And there was no shortage of eyewitnesses like Holmes to record the wrenching national transfiguration and describe its impact on individuals, North and South. Their impressions explored war in every nuance and from every perspective: those of heroes, victims, stoics, shirkers, angels of mercy, and those merely struggling to survive. They told of where men fought, how they fought, and, in the rarest and most sublime examples, why they fought.

This book attempts to recreate in brief their many and

varied voices, particularly soldiers in combat and camp who wrote yearningly to wives, sweethearts, and parents of their resolve, suffering, boredom, and jubilation; and the women they left behind, often coping with hunger, deprivation, even degradation. Here are collected the thoughts of letter-writers, dispatch-writers, and diarists, all striving to make sense of the upheavals roiling their lives. A cacophony of voices are raised to advocate state rights and national rights, equality and slavery, the inviolability of Union, and the sacred right of secession— all with equal conviction. Human slaughter and suffering are experienced and evoked in aching detail.

The voices are both military and civilian, black and white, male and female, poor and rich, domestic and foreign. The words come from the pens of journalists and farmers, poets and presidents, preachers and prisoners, abolitionists and bigots, famous generals, and unknown soldiers. Not only are erudite officers like Holmes represented here, but also common soldiers barely able to spell—yet who, their scribbled notes reveal, were no less profoundly absorbed by the conflagration of war. Together they vivify the full scope of America's most tragic conflict—of a family bitterly and brutally at war with itself.

Innumerable sources were consulted to assemble the excerpts for this volume: journals, diaries, memoirs, autobiographies, collected correspondence, original letters, period newspapers, and regimental histories, as well as modern Civil War texts. In the end, the sheer weight of this archive required that far more be omitted than included. Still, it is hoped that these selections—

both familiar and hitherto unknown, representative and exotic—convey the full breadth of the struggle that reshaped America. What may well astonish the modern reader (as it did the editor), even more than the unforgettable scenes many entries describe, is the high style in which some descriptions were composed: educated Americans in the mid-19th century were educated first and foremost to write, and many of them wrote extraordinarily well. Their graphic recollections not only portray the harrowing particulars of life and death in wartime, they illuminate the resolve that steeled their writers to endure and ennoble their sacrifices. In the end, they cannot help but shed light on an otherwise unfathomably tragic conflict.

It might be said that the Oliver Wendell Holmes, Jr., who spoke so wistfully on Memorial Day, 1884, underestimated himself—and his age. In the very impressions that he and his contemporaries once recorded, the supposedly "incommunicable experience of war" did indeed reveal itself in harrowing, often heartbreaking detail. These fighting words of raw emotion and uncanny observation invite modern readers to feel again "the passion of life to its top" that so consumed Holmes—and in the process, nearly consumed an entire nation. Like their authors and their era, these words are surely "touched with fire."

PROLOGUE: A HOUSE DIVIDING

AMERICA'S PAINFUL DESCENT toward disunion and fratricidal war, looming for generations, may have been hastened irreversibly in 1854, when Congress passed a new law called the Kansas-Nebraska Act.

The act overturned the 34-year-old Missouri Compromise, which had restricted slavery to the South. Now an expansion of what John C. Calhoun had called the "peculiar domestic institution" into new western territories suddenly seemed, to many, painfully inevitable. Among other consequences, the new law "aroused" back into politics a former Whig Congressman from central Illinois named Abraham Lincoln.

A bloody fight over whether to admit Kansas to the

Union as a slave state or a free state exacerbated the growing crisis. In the frenzy of sectional passion, an anti-slavery leader was even brutally caned on the floor of the U.S. Senate. Then in 1857 the Supreme Court ruled, in its infamous Dred Scott decision, that blacks were perpetually ineligible for American citizenship, and that Congress was legally powerless to bar slave "property" from any U.S. territory. To anti-slavery leaders, the decision signaled nothing less than a conspiracy to spread the hated institution nationwide.

The following year, the new, anti-slavery Republican party nominated Lincoln as its designee in Illinois to oppose the father of the controversial Kansas-Nebraska Act, two-term Democratic Senator Stephen A. Douglas. Douglas championed the doctrine of "popular sovereignty"—the right of white citizens of each new territory, regardless of geography, to vote slavery up or down for themselves; Lincoln was an outspoken opponent of the spread of slavery anywhere. (Not even Lincoln, it should be noted, then advocated abolishing slavery where it already existed.) Beginning in August 1858, the two candidates hurled invectives at each other in a series of seven acrimonious debates, arguably the most famous such encounters in the history of American politics. Douglas went on to win the election, but Lincoln won a huge new national reputation. Voters emerged more intractably divided than ever.

Over the next two years, Northern and Southern positions hardened, and rhetoric on both sides boiled over. Progressive Northerners warned that denying liberty to slaves threatened to subvert democracy itself. Southerners, further jolted by the ill-fated, sensational military raid into Harpers Ferry, Virginia, by Abolitionist zealot John Brown, insisted that it was *their* liberty—including their right to own slaves—that was in jeopardy. An ominous sign that the body politic had fatally frayed came in 1860, when the traditional two-party system failed to accommodate the discordant mood of the bitterly split electorate.

No fewer than four parties nominated candidates for the Presidency that year, but from the outset, it was a rematch between the battered Illinois warriors of 1858, Lincoln and Douglas. By prevailing in the North—and only the North—Lincoln won the White House, even though he amassed only 40% of the popular vote. Predictably, his sectional victory was greeted in the South as tantamount to a declaration of war, and several states promptly seceded from the Union and formed a new government. The crisis was at fever pitch.

Just as Lincoln had predicted in 1858, the house divided against itself could not stand. And by the time he left Illinois to assume the presidency, it had all but fallen.

. . .

Georgia Congressman Robert Toombs, speech before the U.S. House of Representatives, June 15, 1850:

I stand upon the great principle that the South has right to an equal participation in the territories of the United States. . . . Deprive us of this right and appropriate this common property to yourselves, it is then your government, not mine. Then I am its enemy, and I will then, if I can, bring my children and my constituents to the altar of liberty, and like Hamilcar [a 5th-century B.C. Carthaginian general], I would swear them to eternal hostility to your foul domination. Give us our just rights, and we are ready, as heretofore, to stand by the Union. . . . Refuse it, and for one, I will strike for *Independence*.

The Influence of *Uncle Tom*

"Who was your mother?" "Never had none!" said the child, with another grin. "Never had any mother? What do you mean? Where were you born?" "Never was born," persisted Topsy. "Do you know who made you?" "Nobody, as I knows on," said the child with a short laugh. . . . "I 'spect I grow'd."

—*Harriet Beecher Stowe,* Uncle Tom's Cabin, *1852*

(Stowe's landmark novel sold an astounding 300,000 copies in the United States alone, and aroused renewed and heated debate over the evils of slavery. Liberals praised the book lavishly, while pro-slavery Southerners denounced its author and answered with a spate of sugar-coated, far less influential books. Supposedly, when Abraham Lincoln met Mrs. Stowe a few years later, he proclaimed: "So you're the little woman who wrote the book that made this great war.")

. . .

We have got to hating everything with the prefix *free*, from free negroes up and down through the whole catalogue—*free farms, free labor, free society, free will, free thinking, free children, and free schools*—all belonging to the same brood of damnable *isms*.

—A Virginia editor, quoted in the National Intelligencer, October 21, 1856

It is not alone a fight between the North and the South; it is a fight between freedom and slavery; between God and the devil; between heaven and hell.

—Former Congressman George Washington Julian of Indiana, political address quoted in the National Intelligencer *on the same day, October 21, 1856*

A Supreme Court Landmark

Chief Justice Roger B. Taney, majority opinion in the Dred Scott decision, March 1857:

The question is simply this: Can a negro, whose ancestors were imported into this country and sold as slaves, become a member of the political community formed and brought into existence by the Constitution of the United States, and as such become entitled to all the rights, and privileges, and immunities, guarantied [*sic*] by that instrument to the citizen. . . . He may have all of the rights and privileges of the citizen of a State, and yet not be entitled to the rights and privileges of a citizen in any other State. . . . And upon a full and careful consideration of the subject, the court is of the opinion that, upon the facts stated in the plea in abatement, Dred Scott was not a citizen of Missouri within the meaning of the Constitution of the United States, and not entitled as such to sue in its courts; and, consequently, that the Circuit Court had no jurisdiction of the case, and that the judgment on the plea in abatement is erroneous.

(With this conclusion, the United States Supreme Court denied the slave Dred Scott's claim that he should be freed because his master had taken him from a slave state to a free state. Southerners applauded the ruling; Northerners attacked it. Historians agree that it helped hasten the dissolution of the Union.)

Let the next President be Republican, and 1860 will mark an era kindred with that of 1776.

> —*The Chicago* Tribune, *March 15, 1857, reacting to the Dred Scott decision*

Every Southern man sustains me. The fragments of the stick are begged for as *sacred relics.*

> —*Congressman Preston Brooks of South Carolina, writing two days after he used his cane to beat Charles Sumner of Massachusetts on the Senate floor, May 22, 1857*

(The anti-slavery senator's caning—from which he required three years to recover—outraged Northerners but won high praise throughout the South.)

Abraham Lincoln, June 16, 1858, speech accepting the Republican designation for the U.S. Senate, Springfield, Illinois:

We are now far into the *fifth* year, since a policy was initiated [the Kansas-Nebraska Act], with the *avowed* object, and *confident* promise, of putting an end to slavery agitation. Under the operation of that policy, that agitation has not only, *not ceased*, but has *constantly augmented*. In *my* opinion, it will not cease, until a *crisis* shall have been reached, and passed. "A house divided against itself cannot stand." I believe this government cannot endure, permanently half *slave* and half *free*. I do not expect the Union to be *dissolved*—I do not expect the house to *fall*—but I *do* expect it will cease to be divided. It will become *all* one thing, or *all* the other.

The Great Debate in Illinois

All I have to say is this, if you Black Republicans think that the negro ought to be on a social equality with young wives and daughters, and ride in the carriage with the wife while the master of the carriage drives the team, you have a perfect right to do so . . . [and] those of you who believe that the nigger is your equal, and ought to be on an equality with you socially, politically and legally, have a right to entertain those opinions, and of course will vote for Mr. Lincoln.

—*Stephen A. Douglas, August 27, 1858, debate at Freeport, Illinois*

I am not now nor have I ever been in favor of bringing about in any way, the social and political equality of the white and black races. . . . I do not perceive, however, that because the white man is to have the superior position, that it requires that the negro should be denied everything. I do not perceive because I do not court a negro woman for a wife, that I must necessarily want her for a wife. My understanding is that I can just leave her alone.

—Abraham Lincoln, September 18, 1858, debate at
   Charleston, Illinois

But the Abolition party really think that the Declaration of Independence declared the negroes to be equal to white men—that negro equality is an inalienable right conferred by the Almighty, and hence that all human laws in violation of it are null and void. Well, with such men it is no use for me to argue. I hold that the signers of the Declaration of Independence had no reference to the negro at all, when they declared all men to be created equal. They did not mean negroes nor the savage Indian, nor the Fejee Islander, nor any other barbarous race—they were speaking of white men. . . . I hold that this government was established on the white basis. It was established by white men, for the benefit of white men and their posterity forever, and should be administered by white men and none others. But it does not follow by any means, that merely because a negro is not a citizen, merely because he is not an equal, that therefore he should be a slave.

—*Stephen A. Douglas, October 15, 1858, debate at Alton, Illinois*

That is the real issue! An issue that will continue in this country when these poor tongues of Douglas and myself shall be silent. These are the two principles that are made the eternal struggle between right and wrong. They are the two principles that have stood face to face from the beginning of time; and will ever continue to struggle, one of them asserting the divine right of kings, the same principle that says you work, you toil, you earn bread and I will eat it. It is the same old serpent, whether it comes from the mouth of a king who seeks to bestride the people of his nation, and to live upon the fat of his neighbor, or, whether it comes from one race of men as an apology for the enslavement of another. It is the same old policy.

—*Abraham Lincoln, October 15, 1858, debate at Alton, Illinois*

The Coming Man, Appraised

Mr. Lincoln belongs to that class of politicians who have, for twenty-five years, sought to array one section of the Union against the other. He has recently proclaimed in the Illinois canvas that free and slave labor are incompatible elements in the same government. We like to call things by their right names. Mr. Lincoln is, then, either a shallow empiric, an ignorant pretender, or a political knave. We know nothing of his age and little of his life. . . . If he is not a knave, then he is a very weak, and therefore, as a politician, a very dangerous man.

—The Washington Times, commenting on Lincoln's performance in his debates with Douglas, September 15, 1858

When he touched on the slavery feature of his address, it seemed to me there came an eloquence born of the earnestness of a heart convinced of the sinfulness— the injustice and the brutality of the institution of slavery, which made him a changed man. So long as I live I will never lose the impression he made upon me. It helped strengthen my conviction on the subject of human slavery, and I have heard boys who heard him say that it shaped their opinions and fixed their views in after life. . . . "A house divided against itself cannot stand," said he, "and this nation must be all free or all slave," suiting his words to those of the Christ when he denounced sin and said that sin and unrighteousness could not exist with righteousness in the heart of the same individual.

—Henry Guest McPike, eyewitness to the final Lincoln-Douglas debate at Alton, Illinois, October 15, 1858

. . .

New York Senator William H. Seward, speech at Rochester, New York, October 25, 1858:

Shall I tell you what this collision means? They who think that it is accidental, unnecessary, the work of interested or fanatical agitators, and therefore ephemeral, mistake the case altogether. It is an irrepressible conflict between opposing and enduring forces, and it means that the United States must and will, sooner or later, become either entirely a slave-holding nation or entirely a free-labor nation. . . . I know, and you know, that a revolution has begun.

(Although no more radical than Lincoln's "House Divided" warning four months earlier, Seward's watershed speech aroused far more indignation. The anti-Republican New York *Herald*, for example, denounced its author as an "arch agitator.")

.   .   .

I John Brown am now quite *certain* that the crimes of this *guilty land* will never be purged *away*; but with Blood. I had *as I now think vainly* flattered myself that without *very much* bloodshed it might be done.

—*John Brown, December 2, 1859, final message before his execution, Charles Town, Virginia*

(On October 16, 1859, the Connecticut-born abolitionist—together with 21 armed men—seized the federal arsenal at Harpers Ferry as part of an improbable plot to trigger a slave insurrection in Virginia. Instead he was captured by federal troops under Lt. Col. Robert E. Lee, two days later. He was quickly tried and convicted, and hanged only hours after writing this letter.)

On the Election of Lincoln

The evil days, so dreaded by our forefathers and the early defenders of the Constitution, are upon us. We need not disguise the fact from ourselves, our friends, or our country. . . . The pure hearts of our distinguished Statesmen, who, years ago, saw the cloud no bigger than a man's hand, who prophesied evil to the country from this speck on the political horizon,—those pure hearts, we say, would now tremble at the accumulation of iniquity laid up against this aggressive party, its slow and steady accretions, until the last straw has broken the camel's back, and an outraged and forbearing people stand up in their majesty, and say—*"thus far, and no farther."*

—*The Dallas* Herald, *commenting on the election results of November 6, 1860*

What, then, has been gained to the anti-slavery cause by the election of Mr. Lincoln? Not much, in itself considered, but very much when viewed in the light of its relations and bearings. For fifty years the country has taken the law from the lips of an exacting, haughty and imperious slave oligarchy. The masters of slaves have been masters of the Republic. Their authority was almost undisputed, and their power irresistible. They were the President makers of the Republic, and no aspirant dared to hope for success against their frown. Lincoln's election has vitiated their authority, and broken their power. It has taught the North its strength, and shown the South its weakness. More important still, it has demonstrated the possibility of electing, if not an Abolitionist, at least an *anti-slavery reputation* to the Presidency.

> —*Frederick Douglass, writing in the* Douglass Monthly *on Lincoln's election, November 6, 1860*

Thus is the glorious truth emphasized again, that right at last makes might. Thus have American institutions reinstated themselves in the affections and admirations of the world. The Sovereignty of the people rising in awful majesty has overwhelmed the minions of oligarchical tyranny and slavery propagandism. The fat has gone forth which transfers the sceptre from the nerveless grasp of recreant and degenerate Democracy to another power, in the person of Abraham Lincoln.

> —*The St. Louis* Democrat *on the election of Lincoln, November 6, 1860*

The tea has been thrown overboard, the revolution of 1860 has been initiated.

> —*The Charleston* Mercury, *November 8, 1860, reacting to news of Lincoln's election*

. . . **November 6.** Abraham Lincoln elected President of the United States. . . . .

Hurtling Toward Secession

I think I see in the future a gory head rise above our horizon. Its name is Civil War. Already I can see the prints of his bloody fingers upon our lintels and door-posts. The vision sickens me already.

—Thomas R. R. Cobb, Clerk of the Georgia Supreme
Court, pro-secession speech in Milledgeville, Georgia,
November 12, 1860

Shall we surrender the jewels because their robbers and incendiaries have broken the casket? Is this the way to preserve liberty? I would as lief surrender it back to the British crown as to the abolitionists. I will defend it from both. Our purpose is to defend those liberties. What baser fate could befall us or this great experiment of free government than to have written upon its tomb: "Fell by the hands of abolitionists and the cowardice of its natural defenders." If we quail now, this will be its epitaph.

—Senator Robert Toombs of Georgia, pro-secession
speech in Milledgeville, Georgia, November 13, 1860

(Toombs resigned his U.S. Senate seat, but then lost a bid for the Confederate presidency. He was severely wounded at the

Battle of Antietam. As for Cobb, nearly two years after predict-
ing bloodshed and war in his speech, he was killed in action at
the Battle of Fredericksburg.)

The long-continued and intemperate indifference of
the Northern people with the question of slavery in the
Southern States has at length produced its natural effects ... [but] the election of any one of our fellow-
citizens to the office of President does not itself afford
just cause for dissolving the Union. ... The day of evil
may never come unless we shall rashly bring it upon
ourselves.

> —*President James Buchanan, last Annual Message to
> Congress, December 4, 1860, Washington*

The evil has now passed beyond control, and must be
met by each and all of us, under our responsibility to
God and our country.

> —*Secretary of the Treasury Howell Cobb of Georgia, in
> resigning from the Buchanan cabinet, December 8, 1860*

Let there be no compromise on the question of *extend-
ing* slavery. If there be, all our labor is lost, and, ere long,
must be done again. The dangerous ground—that into
which some of our friends have a hankering to run—is
Pop[ular]. Sovereignty. Have none of it. Stand firm. The
tug has to come, & better now, than any time hereafter.

> —*President-elect Abraham Lincoln to Senator Lyman
> Trumbull, December 10, 1860, Springfield, Illinois*

The First State Secedes

We affirm that these ends for which this Government was instituted have been defeated, and the Government itself has been destructive of them by the action of the non-slaveholding States. Those States have assumed the right of deciding upon the propriety of our domestic institutions; and have denied the rights of property established in fifteen of the States and recognized by the Constitution; they have denounced as sinful the institution of Slavery; they have permitted the open establishment among them of societies, whose avowed object is to disturb the peace of and eloin [*sic*] the property of the citizens of other States. They have encouraged and assisted thousands of our slaves to leave their homes; and those who remain, have been incited by emissaries, books, and pictures, to servile insurrections.

—From the Ordinance of Secession, State of South Carolina, December 20, 1860

The whole city was wild with excitement as the news spread like wild-fire through its streets. Business was suspended everywhere; the peals of the church bells mingling with salvos of artillery from the citadel. Old men ran shouting down the street. Every one entitled to

... **December 18.** Congress considers Crittenden Compromise to avert disunion and war—then rejects it a week later when Lincoln objects ... **December 20.** South Carolina secedes from the Union. . . . .

it appeared at once in uniform. In less than fifteen minutes . . . the principal newspaper of Charleston had placed in the hands of the eager multitude a copy of the Ordinance of Secession. . . . The heart of the people had spoken.

> —Dr. Samuel Wylie Crawford, U.S. Army officer, describing the scene in Charleston after South Carolina voted to secede from the Union, December 20, 1860

1861

FOUR SCORE AND FIVE YEARS after America had declared independence from Great Britain, one *section* of America declared independence from the other. And for the first and only time in our history, Americans began fighting fellow Americans to the death on the battlefields of war.

As the year 1861 got underway, seven states had left or were about to leave the Union. America suddenly had two capitals, two flags, and two presidents—Abraham Lincoln in the North and Jefferson Davis in the South. And in their first official words the seeds of a long and bloody struggle were planted. Lincoln deprecated war but refused to cede federal authority; Davis repudiated federal authority even if it meant war—he wished only that his section be left in peace.

The battle lines were drawn. "In *your* hands, my dissatisfied fellow countrymen, and not in *mine*," Lincoln warned in his inaugural address, "is the momentous issue of civil war."

Southerners took the dare. On April 12, secessionist troops opened fire on Fort Sumter, a federal garrison perched inside the harbor of hostile Charleston, South Carolina. The fort's guns responded, and the ensuing duel continued for 34 hours. When federal forces inside Sumter surrendered, hauled down the American flag, and evacuated the premises, the Civil War was irreversibly under way.

Lincoln called for 75,000 volunteers the next day. But as they marched to the defense of Washington, some were attacked on the streets of Baltimore—a grim warning that the federal government's tenuous hold over Maryland and other border states was more fragile than ever. The border states held for the Union, but by summer, four more Southern states had joined the Confederacy, and Jefferson Davis was asking for 100,000 volunteers to defend it.

The first battle of the war took place at Manassas, Virginia, on July 21, as Union and Confederate forces met in what was widely expected to be a lopsided encounter that would crush the incipient rebellion. Quite the opposite occurred: Confederate troops fought brilliantly, routed Union forces, and drove them back toward Washington in disarray. Suddenly it was clear that the war would last longer and cost more dearly than anyone had predicted.

Over the next half-year, Union and Confederate

forces fought several more times. Northern troops prevailed at Port Royal, South Carolina, but Confederates scored a triumph at Ball's Bluff, Virginia. Lincoln placed Gen. George B. McClellan in command of all Union troops in the east, but the general showed no disposition to mount an offensive that would put down the insurrection. In the South, meanwhile, a forgotten old general his detractors called "Granny" began again to attract public notice: Robert E. Lee.

The year ended with what Lincoln's beleaguered administration least wanted or needed: a foreign crisis. But when Union naval forces on the high seas seized Confederate diplomats en route to England, America's onetime enemy came perilously close to declaring war against Washington. Not until Christmas week did Lincoln finally act to avert the new crisis by releasing the Confederate envoys. A year that began with a shocking challenge to established federal authority ended in embarrassment and disarray for an authority now fully under siege. The Confederacy, meanwhile, seemed closer than ever to international recognition and a successful defense of its newly declared independence.

• • •

The man and the hour have met.

> —William L. Yancey, author of The Alabama Secession
> Ordinance, heralding the arrival of Jefferson Davis
> for his inauguration as President of the Confederate
> States of America, February 16, 1861, Montgomery,
> Alabama

If this country cannot be saved . . . I would rather be assassinated on this spot than to surrender it.

—Abraham Lincoln, speech at Independence Hall,
Philadelphia, Pennsylvania, on Washington's Birthday,
February 22, 1861

In *your* hands, my dissatisfied fellow countrymen, and not in *mine*, is the momentous issue of civil war. The government will not assail *you*. You can have no conflict, without being yourselves the aggressors. *You* have no oath registered in Heaven to destroy the government, while *I* shall have the most solemn one to "preserve, protect and defend" it. I am loth to close. We are not enemies, but friends. We must not be enemies. Though passion may have strained, it must not break our bonds of affection. The mystic chords of memory, stretching from every battle-field, and patriot grave, to every living heart and hearthstone, all over this broad land, will yet swell the chorus of the Union, when again touched, as surely they will be, by the better angels of our nature.

—Abraham Lincoln, First Inaugural Address, March 4,
1861

. . . **January 9.** Mississippi secedes . . . **January 10.** Florida secedes . . . **January 11.** Alabama secedes . . . **January 19.** Georgia secedes . . . **January 26.** Louisiana secedes . . . **February 1.** Texas secedes . . . **February 8.** Convention of Confederate States meets in Montgomery, Alabama, to draft new constitution. . . . .

Fighting Words

Author and Confederate officer John Esten Cooke to J. E. B. Stuart, April 4, 1861:

Remain with the Lincoln humbug and political farce government, you . . . cannot. He's a foreign despotism to you and to me. I'll fight against it if the time for fighting comes. I, with hundreds more.

(Stuart went on to pledge loyalty to the Confederacy, and became one of its leading field generals; Cooke became Stuart's ordnance officer while serving as a wartime correspondent for Southern journals.)

The Honor of the First Shot

Edmund Ruffin, diary entry, April 12, 1861, Charleston, South Carolina:

Capt. Cuthbert had notified me that his company had requested of me to discharge the first cannon to be fired [against Fort Sumter], which was their 64 lb. Columbiad, loaded with shell. . . . Of course I was highly grati-

... **February 9.** Confederate convention elects Jefferson Davis President of the provisional government of the Confederate States of America ... **February 11.** Lincoln begins journey to assume office, making first of many speeches, none of which conciliates the South ... **February 18.** Davis inaugurated provisional President of Confederacy in Montgomery, Alabama ... **March 4.** Lincoln inaugurated President in heavily guarded Washington ... **March 6.** Davis calls for 100,000 troops.................

fied by the compliment & delighted to perform the service—which I did. The shell struck the fort, at the north-east angle of the parapet.

(A famous agricultural theorist and ardent secessionist and defender of slavery, Ruffin was 67 years old when he was given the honor of firing the first shot of the Civil War.)

The War Begins

"Virginius," reporting the attack on Fort Sumter, April 12, 1861, in the Richmond *Daily Dispatch*:

There goes a shell and bursts just over Sumter. Quick flashes of lurid light are seen, and in twenty seconds, the hoarse voice of the dog of war is heard. . . . There goes a shot from the Floating Battery—it strikes. There goes one of [Union defender Maj. Robert] Anderson's shells—it falls near to his terrible adversary. There goes another shot from Anderson's Barbette. I see the white column of smoke rise at the Iron Battery—the very earth shakes . . . all is enveloped in smoke, and I can see neither Sumter nor the Islands.

(Fort Sumter's 127 men—a Union garrison inside the seceded state of South Carolina—resisted bombardment for nearly 34 hours, finally surrendering on April 14. Although the confrontation had enormous symbolic impact, the only casualties of the brief siege fell when, during sur-

. . . **April 12.** Secessionists open fire on Fort Sumter in Charleston, South Carolina.

render ceremonies, the 50th gun in a planned 100-gun salute to the American flag exploded, killing one soldier.)

.   .   .

Mary Boykin Chesnut, wife of former U.S. Senator, later Confederate officer James Chesnut, diary entry, April 12, 1861, Charleston, South Carolina:

I do not pretend to go to sleep. How can I? If [Major Robert] Anderson [commander of Fort Sumter] does not accept terms—at four—the orders are—he shall be fired upon. I count four—St. Michael chimes. I begin to hope. At half-past four, the heavy booming of a cannon. I sprang out of bed. And on my knees—prostrate—I prayed as I never prayed before. There was a sound of stir all over the house—pattering of feet in the corridor—all seemed to be hurrying one way. I put on my double gown and a shawl and went, too. It was to the housetop. The shells were bursting. . . . Certainly fire had begun. The regular roar of cannon—there it was. And who could tell what each volley accomplished of death and destruction. The women were wild, there on the housetop. Prayers from the women and impreca-tions from the men, and then a shell would light up the scene. . . . I was so weak and weary I sat down on some-thing that looked like a black stool. "Get up, you foolish woman—your dress is on fire," cried a man. And he put me out. It was a chimney, and the sparks caught my clothes . . . but my fire had been extinguished before it broke out into a regular blaze.

The Bloodless Waterloo

We have met them and we have conquered.

> —*Gov. Francis W. Pickens of South Carolina, in a speech in Charleston after the surrender of Fort Sumter, April 14, 1861*

The streets of Charleston present some such aspect as those of Paris in the last Revolution. Crowds of armed men singing and promenading the streets, the battle blood running through their veins—that hot oxygen which is called "the flush of victory" on the cheek. . . . Sumter has set them distraught; never such a victory. It is a bloodless Waterloo.

> —*William Howard Russell, writing in the London* Times *of Charleston after the fall of Fort Sumter, April 14, 1861*

Our Southern brethren have done grievously wrong, they have rebelled and have attacked their father's house and their loyal brothers. They must be punished and brought back, but this necessity breaks my heart.

> —*Maj. Robert Anderson, commandant of Fort Sumter, after its surrender, April 14, 1861*

. . . **April 14.** Fort Sumter evacuated by federal troops . . . .

Lincoln Calls for Troops

Whereas the laws of the United States have been for some time past, and now are opposed, and the execution thereof obstructed . . . by combinations too powerful to be suppressed by the ordinary course of judicial proceedings . . . Now therefore I, Abraham Lincoln, President of the United States, in virtue of the power in me vested by the Constitution, and the laws, have thought fit to call forth, and hereby do call forth, the militia of the several States of the Union, to the aggregate number of seventy-five thousand, in order to suppress said combinations, and to cause the laws to be duly executed. . . . And I hereby command the persons composing the combinations aforesaid to disperse, and retire peaceably to their respective abodes within twenty days from this date.

—Proclamation calling for troops, April 15, 1861,
   Washington

Robert E. Lee, to his sister, Anne Marshall, April 20, 1861, Arlington, Virginia:

With all my devotion to the Union, and the feeling of loyalty and duty of an American citizen, I have not been able to make up my mind to raise my hand against my

... **April 15.** Lincoln calls for 75,000 troops to put down rebellion.................

relatives, my children, my home. I have, therefore, re-signed my commission in the Army, and save in defense of my native State (with the sincere hope that my poor services may never be needed) I hope I may never be called upon to draw my sword.

(That same day, Lee sent a formal letter to General-in-chief Winfield Scott, resigning his commission in the United States Army.)

John G. Nicolay and John Hay, Lincoln's private secretaries, recalling the anxious wait for the reinforcement of Washington, April 23, 1861:

The President, almost a giant in physical stature and strength, combined in his intellectual nature a mas-culine courage and power of logic with an ideal sensi-tiveness of conscience and a sentimental tenderness as delicate as a woman's. This Presidential trust which he had assumed was to him not a mere regalia of rank and honor. Its terrible duties and responsibilities seemed rather a coat of steel armor, heavy to bear, and cutting remorselessly to the quick flesh. That one of the suc-cessors of Washington should find himself even to this degree in the hands of his enemies was personally humil-iating.... In others' society he gave no sign of these

... **April 17.** Virginia secedes ... **April 17.** Davis approves privateering against Union shipping ... **April 18.** Union abandons arsenal at Harpers Ferry, Virginia, scene of John Brown's raid in 1859 ... **April 19.** Lincoln imposes blockade against Confederate coast ... **April 19.** Mob attacks 6th Massachusetts Militia as it marches through Baltimore, Maryland, en route to defense of Washington ... **April 20.** Robert E. Lee resigns his commission in the United States Army to return to Virginia........................

inner emotions. But once, on the afternoon of the 23rd, the business of the day being over, the Executive Office deserted, after walking the floor alone in silent thought for nearly half an hour, he stopped and gazed long and wistfully out of the window down the Potomac in the direction of the expected ships; and, unconscious of other presence in the room, at length broke out with irrepressible anguish in the repeated exclamation, "Why don't they come! Why don't they come!"

(Lincoln's secretaries—later his biographers—admitted of these painful hours that Lincoln knew that "for the moment the forces which made the beam vibrate with such uncertainty were beyond his control." New York's 7th Regiment finally arrived two days later.)

Thousands of soldiers are guarding us, and if there is safety in numbers, we have every reason, to feel secure. We can only hope for peace.

—*Mary Lincoln to Mrs. Samuel H. Melvin, an old Springfield friend, April 27, 1861*

Col. Nathan Bedford Forrest, C.S.A., recruiting advertisement, May 1861:

I will receive 200 able-bodied men if they will present themselves at my headquarters by the first of June with a good horse and gun. I wish none but those who desire to

... **April 27.** In a controversial move, Lincoln orders Gen. Winfield Scott to suspend the writ of *habeas corpus* in Maryland ... **May 6.** Arkansas secedes ....

be actively engaged. My headquarters for the present is at Corinth, Miss. Come on, boys, if you want a heap of fun and to kill some Yankees.

(This notice—probably dictated by the semiliterate Forrest but rewritten by an aide or editor—reflected the Confederate officer's belief that "war means fightin' and fightin' means killin'.")

War declared with the South, and our Concord company went to Washington. A busy time getting them ready, and a sad day seeing them off, for in a little town like this we all seem like one family in times like these. At the station the scene was very dramatic, as the brave boys went away perhaps never to come back again. I've often longed to see a war, and now I have my wish. I long to be a man, but as I can't fight, I will content myself with working for those who can.

—*Louisa May Alcott, diary entry, mid-April 1861, Concord, Massachusetts*

(The following year, Alcott became a nurse at a Union hospital in Washington, where she was struck down, soldierlike, by typhoid fever; she later recovered.)

Judith Brockenbrough McGuire, diary entry, May 4, 1861, from her home in Alexandria, Virginia:

Why did we think it necessary to send off all that was so dear to us from our own home? I threw open the shutters, and the answer came at once, so mournfully! I heard distinctly the drums beating in Washington. The evening was so still that I seemed to hear nothing else. As I looked at the Capitol in the distance, I could scarcely believe my senses. The Capitol of which I had always been so proud! Can it be possible that it is no longer *our* Capitol? And are our countrymen, under its very eaves, making mighty preparations to drain our heart's blood?

Mustering Officer Ulysses S. Grant to the Adjutant General of the United States, May 24, 1861, Galena, Illinois:

Having served for fifteen years in the regular army, including four years at West Point, and feeling it the duty of every one who has been educated at the Government expense to offer their services for the support of that Government, I have the honor, very respectfully, to tender my services, until the close of the War, in such capacity as may be offered. I would say that in view of my present age, and length of service, I feel myself competent to command a Regiment if the President, in his judgement, should see fit to entrust one to me.

Abraham Lincoln, message to a special session of Congress, July 4, 1861, Washington:

This is essentially a People's contest. On the side of the Union, it is a struggle for maintaining in the world,

... **May 20.** North Carolina secedes ... **May 24.** Col. E. E. Ellsworth, a Lincoln prodigy, killed in Alexandria, Virginia, after tearing down Confederate flag from Marshall House hotel . . . .

that form, and substance of government, whose leading object is, to elevate the condition of men—to lift artificial weights from all shoulders—to clear the paths of laudable pursuit for all—to afford all, an unfettered start, and a fair chance, in the race of life. . . . Our popular government has often been called an experiment. Two points in it, our people have already settled—the successful *establishing*, and the successful *administering* of it. One still remains—its successful *maintenance* against a formidable internal attempt to overthrow it. It is now for them to demonstrate to the world, that those who can fairly carry an election, can also suppress a rebellion—that ballots are the rightful, and peaceful, successors of bullets; and that when ballots have fairly, and constitutionally, decided, there can be no successful appeal, back to bullets.

Glimpses of War

Today, in the drawing room, saw a vivandière [female attendant of a regiment]—in the flesh. She was in the uniform of her regiment but wore Turkish pantaloons. She frisked about in her hat and feathers—did not uncover as a man would have done—played the piano,

. . . **June 8.** Tennessee secedes . . . **June 11.** Gen. George B. McClellan comes to national attention with victory at small engagement at Rich Mountain, Virginia . . . **July 4.** Lincoln's "This is a People's Contest" message to special session of Congress; asks for 400,000 additional troops . . . .

sang war songs. She had no drum, but she gave us "rat-a-plan." She was followed at every step by a mob of admiring soldiers and boys. Yesterday, as we left the cars, we had a glimpse of war. It was the saddest sight. The memory of it is hard to shake off. Sick soldiers—not wounded. There were quite two hundred (they said), lying about as best they might on the platform. . . . These pale, ghastly faces. So here is one of the horrors of war we had not reckoned on.

—*Mary Boykin Chesnut, diary entry, July 13, 1861, Richmond, Virginia*

Maj. Sullivan Ballou, 2nd Rhode Island, to his wife, Sarah, July 14, 1861, from Camp Clark, Washington, D.C.:

The memories of the blissful moments I have spent with you come creeping over me, and I feel most grateful to God and to you that I have enjoyed them so long. And hard it is for me to give them up and burn to ashes the hopes of future years, when, God willing, we might still have lived and loved together, and seen our sons grown up to honorable manhood, around us. I have, I know, but few and small claims upon Divine Providence, but something whispers to me—perhaps it is the wafted prayer of my little Edgar, that I shall return to my loved ones unharmed. If I do not my dear Sarah, never forget how much I love you, and when my last breath escapes me on the battle field, it will whisper your name. Forgive my many faults, and the many pains I have caused you. . . . But, O Sarah! if the dead can come back to earth and flit unseen around those they loved, I shall always be near you; in the gladdest days and in the darkest nights ... *always, always,* and if there be a soft breeze upon your back, it shall be my breath, as the cool air fans your throbbing temple, it shall be my spirit passing by. Sarah do not mourn me dead; think I am gone and wait for thee, for we shall meet again.

(One week after writing this letter, Ballou was killed at the Battle of Bull Run. Some scholars have called into question the authenticity of this composition, arguing that it was enhanced in later years by professional writers; no one knows for sure.)

William Howard Russell, correspondent for the London *Times*, describing the prelude to the Battle of Bull Run, July 20, 1861:

Every carriage, gig, wagon, and hack has been engaged by people going out to see the fight. ... The French cooks and hotel-keepers, by some occult process of reasoning, have arrived at the conclusion that they must treble the prices of their wines and of the hampers of provisions that the Washington people are ordering to comfort themselves at their bloody Derby.

Charles Carleton Coffin, Boston *Journal*, reporting on the Battle of Bull Run, July 21, 1861:

The trees are splintered, crushed, and broken, as if smitten by thunderbolts. Twigs and leaves fall to the ground. There is smoke, dust, wild talking, shouting; hissings, howlings, explosions. It is a new, strange, unanticipated experience to the soldiers of both armies, far different from what they thought it would be.

A General Rechristened

Look! There is Jackson standing like a stone wall.

—Gen. Barnard E. Bee, at the Battle of Bull Run,
July 21, 1861

(For generations Bee's famous words have been interpreted as a battlefield rallying cry intended to inspire Confederate soldiers on the field. Recently, some scholars have suggested that Bee made his declaration *after* the battle, while lying mortally wounded, furious that Jackson had stood by "like a stone wall" while his own forces were being crushed. Bee died on July 22, but the name he had coined for Gen. Thomas J. Jackson—"Stonewall"—lived on.)

. . .

Numbers of gay members of Congress had come out from Washington to witness the battle from the adjacent hills, provided with baskets of champagne and lunches. So there was a regular chariot race when the rout began. . . . We found, occasionally, along the road, parasols

---

. . . **July 21.** Confederate forces defeat Union at the First Battle of Bull Run, Manassas, Virginia . . . .

and dainty shawls lost in their flight by the frail, fair ones who had seats in most of the carriages of this excursion.

—*W. W. Blackford, aide to Confederate general J. E. B. Stuart, recalling the Union retreat from Bull Run, July 21, 1861*

The Victory of the "Frantic" Confederates

Our men were perfectly frantic. Regiment after regiment ran up the hill in the wild excitement of pursuit. . . . The men shouted, "To Washington," "to Baltimore," &c &c, and I believe, if left to themselves they would have neared the first point, for the enemy were in a perfect rout.

—*Correspondent for the New Orleans True Delta, reporting the Confederate victory at the Battle of Bull Run, July 21, 1861*

(Union forces had been widely expected to rout the enemy at the first battle of the war, near Manassas, Virginia. But after buckling at first under early Union offensives, Southern troops rallied and drove the federals back toward Washington. Union forces lost 2,896 at Bull Run, the Confederates 1,982.)

Today will be known as BLACK MONDAY. We are utterly and disgracefully routed, beaten, whipped by secessionists.

—*Attorney George Templeton Strong, diary entry, July 21, 1861, New York City*

Little did I conceive of the greatness of the defeat, and the magnitude of the disaster.... So short-lived has been the American Union, that men who saw it rise may live to see it fall.

—William Howard Russell, writing in the London Times *of the Union defeat at Bull Run, July 21, 1861*

Failing to Stem Retreat

We called to them, tried to tell them there was no danger, called them cowards, denounced them in the most offensive terms, put out our heavy revolvers and threatened to shoot them, but all in vain; a crazy, mad, hopeless panic possessed them, and communicated to everybody about in front and rear. The heat was awful, although it was now about six; the men were exhausted—their mouths gaped, their lips cracked and blackened with the powder of the cartridges they had bitten off in the battle, their eyes staring in frenzy; no mortal ever saw such a mass of ghastly wretches.

—Ohio Congressman Albert G. Riddle, witnessing the Union retreat from Bull Run, July 21, 1861

Where are the vaunts, and the proud boasts with which you went forth? Where are your banners and your bands of music, and your ropes to bring back prisoners? The sun rises early, but shines not. The men appear, at first sparsely and shamefaced enough, then thicker, in the streets of Washington; appear in Pennsylvania Avenue and on the steps and basement entrances. They come along in disorderly mobs; some in squads, stragglers, companies. Occasionally a rare regiment, in perfect order, with its officers (some gaps, dead—the true braves) marching in silence, with lowering faces—stern, weary to sinking, all black and dirty. . . . Sidewalks of Pennsylvania Avenue, Fourteenth Street, etc., crowded, jammed with citizens, darkies, clerks, everybody, lookers-on; women in the windows; curious expressions from faces, as those swarms of dirt-covered returned soldiers . . . move by; but nothing said, no comments; (half our lookers-on Secesh of the most venomous kind—they say nothing, but the devil snickers in their faces).

—*Walt Whitman, writing later in* Specimen Days *about July 23, 1861 in Washington*

. . .

Mary Boykin Chesnut, diary entry, July 24, 1861, Richmond, Virginia:

Mrs. Davis's drawing room last night was brilliant, and she was in great force. Outside a mob collected and called for the president. He did speak. He is an old warhorse—and scents the battlefields from afar. His enthusiasm was contagious. The president took all the credit to himself for the victory [at Bull Run]—said the wounded roused and shouted for Jeff Davis and the men rallied at the sight of him and rushed on and routed the enemy. The truth is, Jeff Davis was not two miles from the battlefield, but he is greedy for military fame.

Private Allen A. Kingsbury, First Massachusetts Infantry, to his parents, July 25, 1861, Arlington Heights, Virginia, recalling wounds suffered at Bull Run four days earlier:

A perfect volley of rifle shot . . . rained around me; one bullet struck me on the breast, went through my blanket and hit the eagle on my cross belt, and knocked me down. Another ball cut off my cap box. . . . The balls fell like hailstones around us, but I did not mind them; was as cool as ice. When I had got out of the woods and was walking along, a cannon ball struck the ground about a rod behind me, and rebounding, hit me in the joint of the knee, upon the under side, and knocked me down. I did not know where I was for several minutes. When I got up I could not stand. Two of the N.Y. 69th took me up and carried me to the wagons. I did not think I was hurt much, but I found I could not walk, so I was carried to the hospital at Centreville, where I staid till Sunday, when I went out to join my Co., but they would not let me, so I remained with the wagons. . . . I am quite lame now, so that I don't go round much. I do not know what they will do with me. *I shall try to get home* if I can. No more this time. *Don't worry about me!* Love to all.

(Kingsbury was sent home to recuperate, as he hoped, but returned to the service the following spring. Shortly thereafter, during the Peninsular Campaign, the Army of the Potomac's campaign along the Virginia peninsula toward Richmond, he was killed in action.)

. . . **July 27.** Lincoln names McClellan commander of Department of Potomac . . . .

Rose O'Neal Greenhow, recalling her arrest by Union troops, Washington, August 1861:

Men rushed with frantic haste into my chamber, into every sanctuary. My beds, drawers, and wardrobes were all upturned; soiled clothes were pounced upon with avidity, and mercilessly exposed; papers that had not seen the light for years were dragged forth. My library was taken possession of, and every scrap of paper, every idle line was seized, even the torn fragments in the grates or other receptacles were carefully gathered together by these latter-day insurrectionists.

(The widow Greenhow, well known in Washington social circles when war broke out, was said to have provided the Confederacy with vital military secrets that helped defeat the Union at Bull Run in July. She was first arrested in August 1861, then tried and deported to Richmond in the spring of 1862. Unrepentant to the end, she was lionized in the postwar South.)

Brig. Gen. N. B. Pearce, C.S.A., recalling preparations for the Battle of Wilson's Creek, Missouri, August 10, 1861:

The scene of preparation, immediately following the orders so long delayed and now so eagerly welcomed by the men, was picturesque and animating in the extreme. . . . Here, a group would be molding bullets—there, another crowd dividing percussion-caps, and, again, another group fitting new flints to their old muskets. They had little thought then of the inequality between the discipline, arms, and accoutrements of the regular United States troops they were soon to engage in battle, and their own homely movements and equipments. It was a new thing to most of them, this regular way of shooting by word of command, and it was, perhaps, the old-accustomed method of using rifle, musket or shot-gun as gamesters or marksmen that won them the battle when pressed into close quarters with the enemy.

(The Union lost 24% of its men to the Confederates' 12% during this first major battle in the west.)

His First Taste of Command

Gen. Ulysses S. Grant, probably August 17, 1861, near Palmyra, Missouri:

My sensations as we approached what I supposed might be "a field of battle" were anything but agreeable. I had been in all the engagements in Mexico that it was possible for one person to be in; but not in command. If some one else had been colonel and I had been lieutenant-colonel I do not think I would have felt any trepidation. Before we were prepared to cross the Mississippi River at Quincy my anxiety was relieved; for the men of the besieged regiment came straggling into town. I am inclined to think both sides got frightened and ran away. . . . As we approached . . . my heart kept getting higher and higher until it felt to me as though it was in my throat. I would have given anything then to have been back in Illinois, but I had not the moral courage to halt and consider what to do. I kept right on.

Private Enoch Colby, First Illinois Light Artillery, to his mother, August 25, 1861, Camp Defiance, Cairo, Illinois:

Mother, I shall strictly abstain from taking anything strong to drink. As for card playing, you know I do not play any more, so I think I shall come out of the war as moral as I went in.

Mary Boykin Chesnut, diary entry, August 29, 1861, Richmond, Virginia:

Our women are now in a nice condition—traveling, your false hair is developed & taken off to see if papers are rolled in it—& you are turned up instantly to see if you have pistols concealed—not to speak of their having women to examine if you are a *man*—in disguise. I think *these* times make all women feel their humiliation in the affairs of the world. With *men* it is on to the field— "glory, honour, praise, &c, power." Women can only stay at home—& every paper reminds us that women are to be *violated*—ravished & all manner of humiliation. How are the daughters of Eve punished.

· · ·

... **August 30.** Gen. John Charles Frémont, U.S.A., issues order confiscating all property of rebels—including slaves—in Missouri; Lincoln orders him to rescind it ....

Private Ovando J. Hollister, First Regiment of Colorado
Volunteers, September 10, 1861, Colorado Territory:

At our first camp on St. Vrain's Creek, a dispute occurred in the party as to whether bacon, used to oil firearms, would or would not make them rust. Little Hawley had ten dollars that said bacon grease was the best that could be used. Jude, on the other side, would bet ten dollars, but he had not got it with him. He put up five—the balance to be staked at the time of trial. As soon as the money was up, the crowd adjourned to an adjoining grocery, procured two buckets of milk and a gallon of whisky, and bound the bet by drinking the stakes. The betters joined us, and as neither ever mentioned it again, the merits of the case are still in the dark.

Private Enoch Colby, First Illinois Light Artillery, to his mother,
September 16, 1861, Paducah, Kentucky:

A good many of the Company have not got any weapons. I have got a revolver and an old cheese knife.

Private Oliver Willcox Norton, U.S.A., to "Friend P—",
October 9, 1861, Camp Leslie, near Falls Church, Virginia:

The first thing in the morning is drill, then drill, then drill again. Then drill, drill, drill, a little more drill. Then drill, and lastly, drill. Between drills, we drill, and sometimes stop to eat a little and have a roll-call.

Dr. William G. Shepardson, writing in the Richmond *Daily Dispatch*, October 9, 1861:

A fine tenor voice commenced singing a low ditty under the window of a fair-faced girl. . . . The sash was thrown up and the fair face testified her pleasure by her appearance on the stage. A crowd began to collect around, and the young man went on from song to song, gaining in confidence and enthusiasm every moment. . . . But there were those among the listeners who did not appreciate the music as much as we did, for a soldier interrupted the song by shouting at the top of his voice: "He's a married man! He's a married man!" This sudden descent from the sublime to the ridiculous changed the scene completely. In popped the fair face; down crashed the window; the wicked soldier laughed all the way from his boots, and the mortified minstrel ended his tenor solo in basso curses.

(The author, who wrote for several Southern journals during the war—calling himself "Bohemian" in his reports for the Richmond paper—observed this amusing scene in Fairfax, Virginia, after a concert performance by the First Virginia Regiment band.)

Private Enoch Colby, First Illinois Light Artillery, to his mother, October 10, 1861, Paducah, Kentucky:

Your fears in regard to my becoming ensnared by designing women need not trouble you in the least. I detest the whole of them and shall *never* associate with them.

Private Randolph A. Shotwell, 8th Virginia Infantry, October 21, 1861, Ball's Bluff, Virginia:

Then ensued an awful spectacle! A kind of shiver ran through the huddled mass upon the brow of the cliff; it gave way; rushed a few steps; then, in one wild, panic-stricken herd, rolled, leaped, tumbled over the precipice! The descent is nearly perpendicular, with ragged, jutting crags, and a water-laved base. Screams of pain and terror filled the air. Men seemed suddenly bereft of reason; they leaped over the bluff with muskets still in their clutch, threw themselves into the river without divesting themselves of their heavy accoutrements, hence went down to the bottom like lead.

(The Union debacle at Ball's Bluff—at which hundreds of soldiers were drowned fleeing the Confederates—horrified the North.)

Gen. George B. McClellan to his wife, Mary Ellen, November 17, 1861, Washington, D.C.:

I went to the White House shortly after tea where I found "the *original gorilla*," about as intelligent as ever. What a specimen to be at the head of our affairs now . . . was of course much edified by his anecdotes—ever apropos, & ever unworthy of one holding his high position.

.   .   .

... **October 21.** Confederates defeat Union at Battle of Ball's Bluff, Virginia; Lincoln intimate, Col. Edward D. Baker, killed in action . . . .

Col. John Singleton Mosby to his wife, November 21, 1861:

After the fight was over I went & looked at the man I killed—the bullet had passed entirely through his head—Font Beattie [one of Mosby's men] got 26 & ¼ dollars out of his pocket—also a nice gold pen & holder (I write this letter with it).

(Mosby, well read and rather refined in civilian life, was completely ruthless as a partisan ranger. This may be the only known letter unashamedly written with a wartime victim's pen by his own killer.)

Gen. Robert E. Lee to his daughters, November 22, 1861, Savannah, Georgia:

I wish I could see you, be with you, and never again part from you. God only can give me that happiness. I pray for it night and day. But my prayers, I know, are not worthy to be heard.

(Still months away from battlefield glory and national fame, Lee was at the time overseeing the Confederate coastal defenses in South Carolina and Georgia.)

. . . **October 24.** Lincoln removes Frémont from command in Missouri . . . **November 1.** McClellan named commander of entire Union army . . . **November 7.** Union captures Port Royal, South Carolina . . . **November 8.** Union navy seizes Confederate Commissioners aboard steamship *Trent*; ensuing "Trent Affair" threatens to bring England into war against Union until Lincoln Administration releases envoys at end of year.

William A. Jones, free black Ohioan, to U.S. Secretary of War
Simon Cameron, November 27, 1861, Oberlin:

Very many of the colored citizens of Ohio and other
states have had a great desire to assist the government in
putting down this injurious rebellion. . . . They have
urged me to write and beg that you will receive one or
more regiments (or companies) of the colored of the
free States to counterbalance those employed against
the Union by Rebels. We are partly drilled and would
wish to enter active service immediately. We behold your
sick list each day and Sympathize with the Soldiers and
the government. We are confident of our ability to stand
the hard Ships of the field and the climate So unhealthy
to the Soldiers of the *North*. To prove our attachment
and our will to defend the government we only ask a
trial[.]

(The Union was not yet prepared to enlist black troops to put
down the Rebellion. This plea was ignored.)

Capt. A. M. Beatty, 4th Pennsylvania Cavalry, recalling his first
glimpse of Lincoln, winter 1861–1862:

Was during the Grand review of McClellands [*sic*]
Army. Being on guard duty and off trick a number of us
privates went over into Columbia heights where the review was to take place to see the manuvers [*sic*]. A
carriage stopped near where we were congregated, and
a long lank man in Citizens clothes, frock coat stovepipe
hat got out, seemed to shake down his pantaloon legs

and get settled into the rest of his clothes. The boys pressed forward, when the word was passed, "That's the President." "That's old Abe." It needed no telling, for he was true to the pictures his friends had given of him. A staff Officer or Aide came rushing up ordering us back. But the President said "Maj[or] let them come up." We passed along in a semblance of order. And Mr. Lincoln grasped the hand of each one. . . . The impression made on me at that time as I took his large bonny [sic] hand in mine and looked in that worn and anxious face with the kindly love-light of those large beautifull eyes remained with me daily.

(Lincoln almost never left Washington during his presidency, except to confer with generals in the field and review troops.)

Gen. Robert E. Lee to his wife, Mary, December 25, 1861, Coosawhatchie, South Carolina:

I cannot let this day of greatful [sic] rejoicing pass, dear Mary, without some communion with you. I am thankful for the many among the past that I have passed with you, & the remembrance of them fills me with pleasure. For those on which we have been separated we must not repine. If it will make us more resigned & better prepared for what is in store for us, we should rejoice. If we can only become sensible of our transgressions, so as to be fully penitent & forgiven, that this heavy punishment under which we labour may with justice be removed from us & the whole nation, what a gracious consummation of all that we have endured it will be!

Private Dan Holmes, First Kansas Cavalry, letter home,
December 30, 1861, Morristown, Missouri:

I don't know how the report of my being killed could
of started. *I believe I am alive.*

(A few months after writing this letter, Holmes was killed in
action.)

1862

THE SECOND YEAR OF THE CIVIL WAR proved a year of genuine revolution—on the battlefield and home front alike.

First, the iron age was dramatically born at sea when the ironclad warships *Monitor* and *Merrimac* dueled off Hampton Roads in Virginia on March 9. The day before, the Confederate *Merrimac* had inflicted the kind of destruction against the Union's wooden navy that would not be endured again until the Japanese attack on Pearl Harbor nearly 80 years later. After the historic meeting between the ironclads, naval warfare was never the same again.

Perhaps the most significant revolution of the entire war was launched on September 22, when President Lincoln announced his preliminary Emancipation Proclamation, giving the rebellious states 100 days, until January 1, 1863, to return to the Union or forfeit their slave property forever. Long an opponent of slavery, but fearful that northern public opinion would not sustain an act of philanthropic liberation, Lincoln finally concluded that he might couch emancipation as a war measure from the commander-in-chief, meant to deprive the enemy of their labor force at home.

Lincoln had actually drafted an emancipation order in July, but this was during the Union army's plodding, ill-fated campaign to capture Richmond. His advisors urged the President to table his proclamation until it could be supported by a military victory. On September 17, the Army of the Potomac obliged by defeating the Army of Northern Virginia at the Battle of Antietam, thus ending a dangerous Confederate invasion of the North. The victory was incomplete—Lincoln was disappointed that his forces did not pursue the enemy army and attempt to destroy it—but it was sufficient to justify his bombshell announcement. Not surprisingly, it created an uproar—not only in the South, but in the North. To a New York artist inspired to immortalize its announcement on canvas, it was nothing less than "an act unparalleled for moral grandeur in the history of mankind." But countless Northerners greeted the Proclamation with outright hostility. The British press accused the President of acting to incite a "servile war." A discouraged Lincoln admitted a week later that "stocks have declined, and troops come forward more slowly than ever . . . not very satisfactory."

Little noticed by the public, by comparison, was another revolutionary proclamation Lincoln issued two days later, suspending the writ of *habeas corpus* nation-wide. It was a temporary sacrifice of constitutionally protected civil liberty that was necessary, Lincoln argued, to save the constitution itself during civil war.

The year ended with a major military triumph by the Confederacy. A reckless Union charge up the impregnable heights above Fredericksburg, Virginia, resulted in a wholesale slaughter of federal troops. By year's end, the war seemed no nearer a conclusion than it had the year before. But Lincoln was not ready to capitulate. "*We* cannot escape history," he told Congress in his annual message on December 1. "In *giving* freedom to the *slave*, we *assure* freedom to the *free*."

Black leader Frederick Douglass, address in Philadelphia, Pennsylvania, January 14, 1862:

I have often been asked since this war began, why I am not at the South battling for freedom. My answer is with the Government. The Washington Government wants men for its army, but thus far, it has not had the boldness to recognize the manhood of the race to which I belong. It only sees in the slave an article of commerce—a contraband. . . . Now, what is the remedy for all this? The answer is ready. Have done at once and forever with the wild and guilty phantasy that any one man can have a right of property in the body and soul of another man. Have done with the now exploded idea that the old Union, which has hobbled along through seventy years upon the crutches of compromise, is either desirable or possible, now, or in the future. Accept the incontestible truth of the "irrepressible conflict". . . . To let this occasion pass unimproved, for getting rid of slavery, would be a sin against unborn generations.

One General's Credo

Git thar fustest with the mostest.

—*Attributed to Gen. Nathan Bedford Forrest, ca. 1862*

(Forrest, an ill-educated professional slave trader from Tennessee, joined the Confederate army and became such a remarkable tactician and leader of men that longtime foe William T. Sherman declared him, at war's end, "the most remarkable man our Civil War produced on either side.")

Brig. Gen. Ulysses S. Grant to Confederate General Simon Bolivar Buckner, February 16, 1862, near Fort Donelson, Tennessee:

Yours of this date, proposing armistice and appointment of Commissioners to settle terms of capitulation, is just received. No terms except unconditional and immediate surrender can be accepted. I propose to move immediately upon your works.

(Buckner quickly accepted "the ungentlemanly and unchivalrous terms which you propose." Fort Donelson on the

Cumberland River fell to the Union, and within a week, so did the western part of Tennessee and all of Kentucky.)

Jefferson Davis, inaugural address as President of the Confederate States of America, February 22, 1862, Richmond, Virginia:

The tyranny of an unbridled majority, the most odious and least responsible form of despotism, has denied us both the right and the remedy. Therefore we are in arms to renew such sacrifices as our fathers made to the holy cause of constitutional liberty.

Richmond belle Constance Cary, recalling the Davis inauguration, February 22, 1862:

It was thought ominous afterwards, when the story was repeated, that, as Mrs. Davis, who had a Virginia negro for a coachman, was driven to the inauguration, she observed the carriage went at a snail's pace and was escorted by four negro men in black clothes, wearing white cotton gloves and walking solemnly, two on either side of the equipage. She asked the coachman what such a spectacle could mean, and was answered, "Well, ma'am, you tole me to arrange everything as it should be; and this is the way we do in Richmond at funerals and sich-like."

... **February 6.** Union, under Admiral Andrew Foote, captures Fort Henry, Tennessee ... **February 16.** Gen. Ulysses S. Grant demands and wins "unconditional surrender" of Fort Donelson, Tennessee ... **February 22.** Davis inaugurated President of the Confederacy in Richmond, Virginia ....

The Union Flag Returns to Nashville

No attempt was made by the enemy to cross the river for another week, when thirty transports under protection of ten gun-boats, commanded by Gen. [William] Nelson [of the Army of the Ohio], came crawling up the Cumberland slowly as though each bluff was a masked battery, and every mile of water a net work of torpedoes. The skies, as if in sympathy, covered the whole face of the country with water. What remained to grace the triumph of a conqueror was only some old men, women and children, with a few Confederate soldiers, too sick to follow their commands. It was a silent surrender with no exclamations of triumph or display of pageant. The Union flag was raised on the Capitol building.

—*Miss "A. M. B.," February 25, 1862, Nashville, Tennessee*

(The writer went on to volunteer in local military hospitals, but her unreconstructable Confederate sympathies soon got her into trouble: she was charged with being a "Rebel letter carrier"—a spy—and arrested. The Union remained in control of Nashville for the rest of the war.)

U.S. Secretary of the Navy Gideon Welles, in his diary, March [9] 1862:

When intelligence reports reached Washington on Sunday morning, the 9th of March, that the Merrimac

---

... **February 25.** Union occupies Nashville, Tennessee ....

had come down from Norfolk and attacked and destroyed the Cumberland and Congress, I called at once on the President . . . [who] was so excited that he could not deliberate or be satisfied with the opinions of non-professional men, but ordered his carriage and drove to the navy yard to see and consult with Admiral Dahlgren and other naval officers, who might be there. . . . But the most frightened man on that gloomy day, the most so I think of any during the Rebellion, was the Secretary of War [Edwin M. Stanton]. He was at times almost frantic. . . . The Merrimac, he said, would destroy every vessel in the service, could lay every city on the coast under contribution, could take Fortress Monroe; McClellan's mistaken purpose to advance to the Peninsula must be abandoned, and Burnside would inevitably be captured. Likely the first movement of the Merrimac would be to come up the Potomac and disperse Congress, destroy the Capitol and public buildings; or she might go to New York and Boston and destroy those cities. . . . Stanton made some sneering inquiry about this new vessel the Monitor, of which he admitted he knew little or nothing.

(The day after the *Merrimac's* first, deadly strike against the federal fleet, a Union ironclad joined the fight at Hampton Roads. The *Monitor's* success in holding off the Confederate vessel allayed the fears of official Washington after what was arguably its darkest day of panic.)

. . . **March–August.** McClellan conducts ill-fated Peninsular Campaign in Virginia, with goal of capturing Richmond . . . **March 8.** Worst U.S. naval disaster until Pearl Harbor as Confederate ironclad *Merrimac* (or *Virginia*) goes on rampage against wooden federal fleet off Hampton Roads, Virginia . . . .

Lt. William F. Keeler, acting paymaster, aboard the U.S.S. *Monitor*, March 9, 1862, Hampton Roads, Virginia:

I experienced a peculiar sensation; I do not think it was fear, but it was different from anything I ever knew before. We were enclosed in what we supposed to be an impenetrable armor—we knew that a powerful foe was about to meet us—ours was an untried experiment and our enemy's fire might make a coffin for us all. Then we knew not how soon the attack would commence, or from what direction it would come, for with the turret, no one of us could see her. The suspense was awful as we waited in the dim light expecting every moment to hear the crash of our enemy's shot.

Birth of the Iron Age at Sea

When I tell you that within the last few hours I have seen the conclusion of the grand naval fight of the campaign; that I have seen the flame and heard the explosion of the *Congress*; have seen the slanting spars—all that is now visible—of the formidable *Cumberland*, the whilom terror of all these parts . . . that I have seen the splendid *Minnesota* with a breach amidships on her port side as wide as the famous parliamentary gap through which an Irish counselor swore a coach and six might be driven . . . that I have seen the gallant *Virginia* [the *Merrimac*— ed.], rough with honorable scars, shooting along like

. . . **March 9.** The *Monitor* battles the *Merrimac* off Hampton Roads, Virginia, ushering in the iron age at sea . . . .

some huge "Saurian," with a jaunty little Confederate flag at her peak gaily flaunting over a superb "star-spangled" . . . when I tell you all this have I not sketched you a chapter of events that will make the 8th and 9th of March "white stone" days in the calendar of the young republic?

—A soldier-correspondent, reporting in the Petersburg (Va.) Daily Express, March 11, 1862

(The devastation unleashed by the fearsome Confederate ironclad *Merrimac* at Hampton Roads, Virginia, on March 8, 1862, would go unchallenged until the following day—when the Union ironclad *Monitor* fought her to a draw, ushering in the age of the iron fighting ship. The losses suffered by the federal navy on that first day would not be equaled until the Japanese attack on Pearl Harbor nearly 80 years later.)

Shiloh and Its Bloody Aftermath

Retreat? No. I propose to attack at daylight and whip them.

—Gen. Ulysses S. Grant, after the first day's fighting at the Battle of Shiloh, Tennessee, April 6, 1862

(Grant's bold decision to counterattack after the Union's costly and unsuccessful first day of fighting at Shiloh turned

. . . **March 16.** Union abolishes slavery in District of Columbia, offering compensation to slaveholders . . . **April 6–7.** Union, under Gen. Grant, wins major victory at Battle of Shiloh (Pittsburgh Landing), Tennessee . . . .

defeat into victory, but at a cost of some 20,000 killed and wounded on both sides—double the casualties at Bull Run, Pea Ridge, Fort Donelson, and Wilson's Creek combined. Historian James M. McPherson has asserted that "Shiloh launched the country onto the floodtide of total war." Enlisted men, officers, and journalists all recorded the grisly details of the terrible cost of Union victory.)

. . .

The dead and wounded are all around me. The knife of the Surgeon is busy at work, and amputated legs and arms lie scattered in every direction. The cries of the suffering victim, and the groans of those who patiently await for medical attendance, are most distressing to any one who has any sympathy with his fellow man. All day long they have been coming in, and they are placed upon the decks and within the cabins of the steamers, and wherever else they can find a resting place. I hope my eyes may never again look upon such sights.

—Ned Spencer, The Cincinnati Times, after the first day of the battle

The scenes on this field would have cured anybody of war.

—Gen. William T. Sherman, writing home from Shiloh, April 7, 1862

There was no pause in the battle. The roar of the strife was ever heard. The artillery bellowed and thundered, and the dreadful echoes went sweeping down the river, and the paths were filled with the dying and the dead. The sound was deafening, the tumult indescribable. No life was worth a farthing. . . . Death was in the air, and bloomed like a poison-plant on every foot of soil.

—*Junius Henri Browne, New York* Tribune, *April 6, 1862, describing the battle*

I saw an intelligent-looking man with his whole diaphragm torn off. He was holding up nearly all of his viscera with both hands and arms. His face expressed a longing for assistance and an apprehension of fatality.

—*Unidentified Union captain, recalling the Battle of Shiloh, April 6, 1862*

Almost every hill now on both sides looked like a volcano, for the deep mouthed cannon were roaring on every side. Soon the rattle of musketry announced that your vanguard had found the foe. The dark line of men now moved quickly in. After minutes more the volleys of musketry announced that they too had entered the bloody arena. It was really a grand scene now: you could not distinguish a musket shot now, it was one continual roar like the rushing of a storm.

—*John H. Pines, Confederate cavalryman, to his parents, describing his first taste of action at Shiloh, April 7, 1862*

Along the sheltered strip of beach between the river bank and the water was a confused mass of humanity— several thousands of men. They were mostly unarmed; many were wounded; some dead. All the camp-following tribes were there; all the cowards; a few officers. Not one of them knew where his regiment was, nor if he had a regiment. Many had not. These men were defeated, beaten, cowed. They were deaf to duty and dead to shame. A more demented crew never drifted to the rear of broken battalions. They would have stood in their tracks and been shot down to a man by a provost-marshall's guard, but they could not have been urged up that bank. An army's bravest men are its cowards. The death which they would not meet at the hands of the enemy they will meet at the hands of their officers, with never a flinching.

—Sergeant Ambrose Bierce, 9th Indiana Volunteers,
describing a scene at Shiloh, April 7, 1862

Sergeant Ambrose Bierce, 9th Indiana Volunteers, describing the aftermath of Shiloh, April 8, 1862:

The bark of these trees, from the root upward to a height of ten or twenty feet, was so thickly pierced with bullets and grape that one could not have laid a hand on it without covering several punctures. None had escaped. How the human body survives a storm like this must be explained by the fact that it is exposed to it but for a few moments at a time, whereas these grand old trees had had no one to take their places. . . . Knapsacks, canteens, haversacks, distended with soaken and swollen biscuits, gaping to disgorge blankets beaten into the soil by the rain, rifles with bent barrels or splintered stocks, waist-belts, hats and the omnipresent sardine-box—all the wretched debris of the battle still littered the spongy earth as far as one could see, in every direction. Dead horses were everywhere . . . Men? There were men enough; all dead apparently, except one, who lay near where I had halted my platoon to await the slower movement of the line—a Federal sergeant, variously hurt. . . . He lay face upward, taking in his breath in convulsive, rattling snorts, and blowing it out with sputters of froth which crawled creamily down his cheeks, piling itself alongside his neck and ears. A bullet had clipped a groove in his skull, above the temple; from this the brain protruded in bosses, dropping off in flakes and strings. . . . One of my men whom I knew for a womanish fellow, asked if he should put his bayonet through him. Inexpressibly shocked by the cold-blooded proposal, I told him I thought not; it was unusual, and too many were looking.

Gen. Ulysses S. Grant, describing the field of Shiloh after the battle, April 8, 1862:

I saw an open field . . . so covered with dead that it would have been possible to walk across the clearing, in any direction, stepping on dead bodies, without a foot touching the ground.

Past Forts Jackson and St. Philip

It was like the breaking up of the universe with the moon and stars bursting in our midst.

> —*Unidentified naval officer aboard the U.S.S.* Hartford,
> *April 24, 1862*

(Farragut's fleet ran the gauntlet between the two Confederate forts on the Mississippi River amid fire so withering it seemed, the admiral admitted, "as if all the artillery of heaven were playing upon the earth.")

A Union officer watching the passage by Farragut's fleet, April 24, 1862:

Combine all that you have heard of thunder, add to it all that you have ever seen of lightning, and you have, perhaps, a conception of the scene.

Come, sir, this is no time for prayer.

> —*Admiral David G. Farragut to journalist Bradley S. Osbon,*
> *who was kneeling on the deck of the Union flagship*
> *before the Battle of New Orleans, April 24, 1862*

(Osbon insisted in his report of this incident that he was merely kneeling to uncap stray shells that had rolled to one side of the deck.)

. . . **April 16.** Davis signs Confederate conscription act . . . **April 24.** Union fleet, under Admiral David Farragut, storms past Forts Jackson and St. Philip on Mississippi River.

Scarcities at Yorktown

The contents of two quart bottles and two pint boxes comprised the medical stores of many commands and were administered as a specific for all complaints. I have seen a surgeon give medicine from the same cup for a sore throat and a scalded foot.

—Capt. Henry N. Blake, 11th Massachusetts Volunteers,
recalling the Union siege of Yorktown, Virginia,
ca. May 1, 1862

(The Confederates eventually abandoned Yorktown, but not before welcoming massive reinforcements and withdrawing to improved positions. Gen. George B. McClellan's decision to lay siege to the town—when he outnumbered its defenders ten to one, and probably could have overrun it if he had attacked—hopelessly bogged down his doomed Peninsular Campaign to capture Richmond.)

"We are all men"

This is a dreadful war to make even the hearts of women so bitter! I, who have such a horror of bloodshed, consider even killing in self-defense murder, who cannot wish them [Union forces occupying her city] the slight-

... **April 25.** Farragut captures New Orleans ... **May 3.** Confederates abandon Yorktown, Virginia, after Union siege led by Gen. McClellan ... **May 5.** Battle of Williamsburg, Virginia ... **May 8.** Confederates win skirmish at McDowell, Virginia, under Gen. Stonewall Jackson ....

est evil, whose only prayer is to have them sent back in peace to their own country, *I* talk of killing them! for what else do I wear a pistol and carving knife? I am almost afraid I *will* try them on the first one who says an insolent word to me. Yes, and repent for ever after in sack cloth and ashes! O if I was only a man! Then I would don the breeches, and slay them with a will! If some Southern women were in the ranks, they would set the men an example they would not blush to follow! Pshaw! There are *no* women here. We are *all* men.

—Sarah Morgan, diary entry, May 9, 1862,
Baton Rouge, Louisiana

· · ·

Julia LeGrand, diary entry, May 9, 1862, New Orleans, Louisiana:

This city, the most important one in the Confederacy, has fallen, and Yankee troops are drilling and parading in our streets. Poor New Orleans! What has become of all your promised greatness! In looking through an old trunk, I came across a letter to my father from my Uncle Thomas, in which, as far back as 1836, he prophesied a noble future for you. What would he say now to see you dismantled and lying low under the heel of an invader!

· · ·

. . . **May 15.** Confederates win naval battle at Drewry's Bluff on James River, near Richmond . . . **June 1.** Davis names Lee commander of Army of Northern Virginia . . . **June 6.** Union captures Memphis, Tennessee . . . **June 12–16.** Gen. J.E.B. Stuart leads daring cavalry raid around McClellan's army; death and martyrdom of Confederate Captain William Latane. . . . .

Correspondent for the Richmond *Daily Dispatch*, June 16, 1862:

We have been in the saddle from Thursday morning until Saturday noon, never breaking rein nor breaking fast; we have whipped the enemy wherever he dared to appear, never opposing more than equal forces; we have burned 200 wagons laden with valuable stores, sunk or fired three large transports, captured 300 horses and mules, lots of side-arms &c, brought in 170 prisoners, four officers, and many negroes, killed and wounded scores of the enemy—pleased [General J. E. B.] Stuart and had one man killed—poor Capt. Latane! This is the result, and $3,000,000 cannot cover the Federal loss in goods alone.

(Jeb Stuart's daring cavalry raid around Union General George B. McClellan's invading army in northern Virginia exhilarated the Confederacy. The sole casualty of the operation, William Latane, became an instant martyr when Union forces refused to allow his brother to transport his body home for burial. Latane's corpse was taken to the nearest plantation, where strangers lovingly interred him in the family plot—an instance of gallantry that inspired a painting, a wildly popular engraving, and a widely performed poem, an excerpt from which follows:)

Let us not weep for him, whose deeds endure,
So young, so brave, so beautiful; he died
As he had wished to die—the past is sure.
Whatever yet of sorrow may betide

Those who still linger by the stormy shore,
    Change cannot touch him now, or fortune harm him
more.

And when Virginia, leaning on her spear—
    "Victrix et Vidua," *the conflict done—*
Shall raise her mailed hand to wipe the tear
    That starts as she recalls each martyred son,
No prouder memory her breast shall sway
    Than thine, our early lost, lamented LATANE.

—John R. Thompson, *in the* Southern Literary Messenger

F. F. Kiner, Union chaplain, on life at Camp Oglethorpe Prison, Macon, Georgia, June 24, 1862:

The meal was brought in barrels, or old sugar hogsheads; the meat was thrown out upon the ground and literally crawled with maggots. They put guards around these rations till they were issued, and we often told them it was necessary to guard it to keep it from crawling off. Some of these hams and sides of meat were so badly spoiled that we could push a finger through and through them, as if they were mince meat. In fact, that was what was the matter with it, the worms had minced it too much. It had spoiled mostly from want of salt, for the grease we got from it was not salt enough to use for gravy. Of this rotten stuff, we got one half pound to the man per day. The maggots upon it

. . . **June 19.** U.S. Congress abolishes slavery in federal territories . . . .

were of the largest kind; perhaps I should call them skippers, for they could skip about and jump several feet at one leap; from their size I judged the climate agreed with them. There was, however, a kind much smaller, which worked into the meat, though it looked middling good, similar to those in cheese, and we could not see them until the meat was cooked, when they made their appearance on the top of the water in the pot, and floated around like clever sized grains of rice.

Private Oliver Norton, 83rd Pennsylvania Volunteers, describing the Battle of Gaines's Mill, Virginia, June 27, 1862:

I was blazing away at the rascals not ten rods off when a ball struck my gun just above the lower band as I was capping it, and cut it in two. The ball flew in pieces and part went by my head to the right and three pieces struck just below my left collarbone. The deepest one was not over half an inch, and stopping to open my coat I pulled them out and snatched a gun from Ames in Company H as he fell dead. Before I fired this at all a ball clipped off a piece of the stock, and an instant after another struck the seam of my canteen and entered my left groin. I pulled it out . . . more maddened than ever . . . [and] in the road a buckshot struck me in the left eyebrow, making the third slight scratch I received in the action. It . . .

. . . **June 25.** Commencement of Seven Days Battles near Richmond . . . **June 26.** Battle of Mechanicsville (Beaver Dam Creek), Virginia . . . **June 27.** Battle of Gaines's Mill (First Cold Harbor), Virginia . . . .

was almost a miracle. . . . Tuesday . . . on the field I picked up a tent and slung it across my shoulder. The folds of that stopped a ball that would have passed through me. I picked it out, put it in my pocket, and, after firing sixty rounds of my own and a number of wounded comrades' cartridges, I came off the field unhurt, and ready, but not anxious, for another fight.

. . .

Private Carlton McCarthy, Richmond Howitzers, Cutshaw's Battalion Artillery, ca. June 30, 1862, near Richmond, Virginia:

During the seven days' battles around Richmond, a studious private observed the rats as they entered and emerged from a corn-crib. He killed one, cooked it privately, and invited a friend to join him in eating a fine squirrel. The comrade consented, ate heartily, and when told what he had eaten, forthwith disgorged. But he confesses that up to the time when he was enlightened he had greatly enjoyed the meal.

Gen. D. H. Hill, C.S.A., at the Battle of Malvern Hill, Virginia, July 1, 1862:

I never saw anything more grandly heroic than the advance after sunset of the nine brigades under [Con-

... **June 29.** Battle of Savage's Station, Virginia . . . **June 30.** Battle of White Oak Swamp (Glendale), Virginia . . . **July 1.** Battle of Malvern Hill, Virginia; McClellan's army retreats to Harrison's Landing, as Peninsular Campaign ends in failure. . . . .

federate Gen. John B.] Magruder's orders. . . . As each brigade emerged from the woods, from fifty to one hundred guns opened upon it, tearing great gaps in its ranks; but the heroes reeled on—and were shot down. . . . It was not war—it was murder.

(Hill is remembered as one of the few Confederate field generals ever to criticize Robert E. Lee—criticism he never withdrew.)

Nathaniel Hawthorne, "Chiefly About War-Matters," July 1, 1862:

It was a platform of iron, so nearly on a level with the water that the swash of the waves broke over it, under the impulse of a very moderate breeze; and on this platform was raised a circular structure, likewise of iron, and rather broad and capacious, but of no great height. It could not be called a vessel at all; it was a machine,—and I have seen one of somewhat similar appearance employed in cleaning out the docks; or, for lack of a better similitude, it looked like a gigantic rat-trap. It was ugly, questionable, suspicious, evidently mischievous,—nay, I will allow myself to call it devilish; for this was the new war-fiend, destined, along with others of the same breed, to annihilate whole navies and batter down old supremacies. The wooden walls of Old England cease to exist, and a whole history of naval renown reaches its period, now that the Monitor comes smoking into view.

Gen. John Pope to his troops, July 24, 1862, on assuming command of the Army of the Potomac:

Let us understand each other. I have come to you from the West, where we have always seen the backs of our enemies.

(Five weeks later at Second Bull Run, Pope's enemies instead saw the backs of Union troops. According to future Union hero Robert Gould Shaw, Pope was nothing more than "a great *blow-hard.*")

"The Furies of Hell" at Second Bull Run

The din was almost deafening, the heavy notes of the artillery, at first deliberate, but gradually increasing in their rapidity, mingled with the sharp treble of the small arms, gave one an idea of some diabolical concert in which all the furies of hell were at work. . . . We do nothing but charge—charge—charge! If the enemy make a bold effort to retrieve the fortunes of the day, (and they made many) and we are repulsed, it is but for the moment, and the regiments rallying upon their supports plunge back again into the tempest of fire that before swept them down. The minie balls which fly in showers seem to bear a death warrant in every devilish

. . . **July 22.** Lincoln reads to his Cabinet a draft emancipation proclamation, is advised to postpone it pending a Union battle victory . . . **August 9.** Gen. John Pope engages Lee at Battle of Cedar Mountain, Virginia . . . **August 29–30.** Lee routs Pope at Second Battle of Bull Run, Manassas, Virginia. . . . .

screech; grape shot and cannister [*sic*] rake the men by scores; friends fall killed and wounded on every hand; shells with their shrill demoralizing shrieks course through the air like fiery monsters, striking where they are least expected, and scattering their fragments in all directions. . . . It was a task of superhuman labor to drive the enemy from these strong points . . . but in less than four hours our indomitable energy had accomplished every thing.

> —*Felix Gregory de Fontaine ("Personnae") writing in the Charleston* Daily Courier *about the Second Battle of Bull Run, Virginia, August 29–30, 1862*

(The Second Battle of Bull Run proved an even more decisive Union rout than the first: the federals lost 16,000 men out of an army of 60,000; 9,200 Confederates fell as well. The victory emboldened Robert E. Lee to invade the North.)

Private David Thompson, 9th New York Volunteers, recalling the Second Battle of Bull Run, August 29–30, 1862:

The truth is, when bullets are whacking against the tree trunks and solid shot are cracking skulls like egg-shells, the consuming passion in the breast of the average man is to get out of the way. Between the physical fear of going forward and the moral fear of turning back, there is a predicament of exceptional awkwardness from which a hidden hole in the ground would be a wonderfully welcome outlet.

Letter published in the New York *Tribune,* commenting on the Union loss at Bull Run, August 29–30, 1862:

This is the plain, unvarnished truth; we have been whipped by an inferior force of inferior men, better handled than our own.

An Historic Commission

Acting upon General Jackson's advice, I removed to Winchester; and it was there and then that I received my commission as Captain and honorary Aide-de-camp to "Stonewall" Jackson; and thenceforth I enjoyed the respect paid to an officer by soldiers. Upon the occasion of a review of the troops in presence of . . . Generals Lee and Longstreet, I had the honor to attend on horseback, and to be associated with the staff officers of several commands.

—*Belle Boyd, September 1862, Martinsburg, Virginia*

(The most notorious of all Confederate spies, Boyd claimed she once ran ten miles to deliver information to Jackson, her hero. Although her claims were probably exaggerated, by the time she wrote this passage she had already been arrested, imprisoned, and exchanged home to the Confederacy. The beautiful spy was dubbed by one Northern newspaper "the Secesh Cleopatra.")

Wanted: Food and Shoes

I look around me and see men barefooted and ragged, bearing only their muskets and a single blanket
each, yet all inspired by the hope of another battle. I
have seen some, too, who were hungry—stragglers
who would come up to the camp fire, tell a pitiful
story of sickness or fatigues [*sic*], and then ask for a
bit of bread and meat. . . . It has become a trite re-
mark among the troops, that "all a Yankee is now
worth is his shoes," and it is said . . . that some of
our regiments have become so expert in securing
these coveted articles, that they can make a charge
and strip every dead Yankee's feet they pass without
coming to a halt. . . .

Writing on a march is not the most convenient or
agreeable task in the world. . . . The shelter of a house is
not to be thought of; a tent is a palace; pen and ink are
tabooed, and a man is forced to seek his epistolary
comfort either at the crumbling end of a lead pencil,
with a shady tree or its equivalent for a sanctum, and
fence rail for his writing desk, or dispense with the same
altogether. . . . It is an ignominious rostrum from which
to talk to twenty thousand people, but it is nevertheless a
fitting illustration of the straits to which all connected
with the army are more or less reduced.

—Felix Gregory de Fontaine ("Personnae"), writing in the
Charleston Daily Courier, from the field, near Brandy
Station, Virginia, September 3, 1862

A. P. Smith, open letter to Abraham Lincoln, September 6,
1862, Saddle River, New Jersey:

Let me tell you, sir, President though you are, there is
but one race of men on the face of the earth:—One lord,
one faith, one baptism, one God and Father of all, who is
above all, and through all, and in all. Physical differences
no doubt there are; no two persons on earth are exactly
alike in this respect; but what of that? In physical conformation, you, Mr. President, may differ somewhat from the
negro, and also from the majority of white men; you may
even, as you indicate, feel this difference on your part to
be very disadvantageous to you; but does it follow that
therefore you should be removed to a foreign country?

(Smith was replying to published comments by the President
to a group of black freedmen at a White House meeting on
August 14. Urging them to recruit families to be colonized in
Central America, Lincoln told his visitors: "There is an un-
willingness on the part of our people, harsh as it may be, for
you free colored people to remain with us. . . . It is better for
us both, therefore, to be separated." Lincoln later backed
away from his colonization scheme, and instead embraced
recruitment of blacks into the Union army.)

The Action at Antietam

From twenty different standpoints great volumes of
smoke were every instant leaping from the muzzles of

. . . **September 4.** Lee's army moves across Potomac River in first Confederate invasion
of the North . . . **September 17.** Battle of Antietam (Sharpsburg), Maryland; Union
forces under McClellan defeat Lee's Confederate troops in bloodiest single day of war.

angry guns. The air was filled with the white fantastic shapes that floated away from bursted shells. Men were leaping to and fro, loading, firing and handling the artillery, and now and then a hearty yell would reach the ear, amid the tumult, that spoke of death or disaster from some well aimed ball. Before us were the enemy. A regiment or two had crossed the river, and running in squads from the woods along its banks, were trying to form a line. Suddenly a shell falls among them and another and another, until thousands scatter like a swarm of flies, and disappear in the woods.

—*Felix Gregory de Fontaine ("Personnae"), writing in the* Charleston *Daily Courier, from Sharpsburg, Maryland, September 17, 1862*

(The Confederate defeat at the Battle of Antietam (known in the South as the Battle of Sharpsburg) effectively ended Lee's first invasion of the North. In the bloodiest day of the Civil War—the bloodiest day American armies ever experienced in any war—26,000 casualties were counted by the two armies, including 4,710 dead. Lee took his exhausted army south, and Union General George McClellan declined to pursue him. Five days later, buoyed by the result, however indecisive, Lincoln issued the Emancipation Proclamation.)

David H. Strother, journalist, describing the Battle of Antietam:

As the smoke and dust disappeared, I was astonished to observe our troops moving along the front and passing over what appeared to be a long, heavy column of the enemy without paying it any attention whatever. I borrowed a glass from an officer, and discovered this to be actually a column of the enemy's dead and wounded lying along a hollow road—afterward known as Bloody Lane. Among the prostrate mass I could easily distinguish the movements of those endeavoring to crawl away from the ground; hands waving as if calling for assistance, and others struggling as if in the agonies of death.

Charles Carleton Coffin, Boston *Journal*, reporting on the Battle of Antietam:

The hillside was dotted with prostrate forms of men in blue, but in the sunken road, what a ghastly spectacle! Confederates had gone down as grass falls before the scythe. Words are inadequate to portray the scene. Resolution and energy still lingered in the pallid cheeks, in the set teeth, in the gripping hand. I recall a soldier with the cartridge between his thumb and finger, the end of the cartridge bitten off, and the paper between his teeth when the bullet had pierced his heart, and the machinery of life—all the muscles and nerves—had come to a standstill. A young lieutenant had fallen while trying to rally his men; his hand was still firmly grasping his sword, and determination was still visible in every line of his face. I counted fourteen bodies lying together, literally in a heap, amid the corn rows on the hillside. The broad, green leaves were sprinkled and stained with blood.

David L. Thompson, 9th New York Volunteers, remembering
the cornfield at Antietam:

In a second the air was full of the hiss of bullets
and the hurtle of grape-shot. The mental strain was
so great that I saw at that moment the singular effect mentioned, I think, in the life of Goethe on a
similar occasion—the whole landscape for an instant
turned slightly red.

Mary Bedinger Mitchell, describing the scene in
Shepherdstown, now West Virginia, across the river from the
Battle of Antietam, September 17, 1862:

We could hear the incessant explosions of artillery,
the shrieking whistles of the shells, and the sharper,
deadlier, more thrilling roll of musketry; while every
now and then the echo of some charging cheer would
come, borne by the wind; and as the human voice
pierced that demoniacal clangor we would catch our
breath and listen, and try not to sob, and turn back to
the forlorn hospitals, to the suffering . . . while imagination fainted at the thought of those other scenes hidden
from us beyond the Potomac. On our side of the river
there were noise, confusion, dust, throngs of stragglers;
horsemen galloping about; wagons blocking each other,
and teamsters wrangling; and a continued din of shouting, swearing, and rumbling, in the midst of which men
were dying, fresh wounded arriving, surgeons amputat-
ing limbs and dressing wounds, women going in and out
with bandages, lint, medicines, food.

Gen. George B. McClellan to his wife, Mary Ellen, September 18, 1862, from camp near Sharpsburg, Maryland:

The spectacle yesterday was the grandest I could conceive of—nothing could be more sublime. Those in whose judgment I rely tell me that I fought the battle splendidly & that it was a masterpiece of art.

(Others disagreed with McClellan's self-aggrandizing conclusion. When the general failed to follow up his advantage after the Battle of Antietam, an exasperated Lincoln finally removed him from command, concluding: "He has got the slows.")

Secretary of the Treasury Salmon P. Chase, diary entry, September 22, 1862, describing the cabinet meeting at which Lincoln decided he would issue the Emancipation Proclamation:

All the members of the Cabinet were in attendance. There was some general talk; and the President mentioned that Artemus Ward [a well-known humorist] had sent him his book. Proposed to read a chapter which he thought very funny. Read it, and seemed to enjoy it very much—the Heads [of federal departments] also (except Stanton) of course. . . . The President then took a graver tone and said—"Gentlemen; I have, as you are aware, thought a great deal about the relation of this war

. . . **September 19.** Union wins Battle of Luka, Mississippi . . . **September 22.** Lincoln issues preliminary Emancipation Proclamation, orders slaves free in all states in rebellion after January 1 . . . .

to Slavery . . . and I have thought all along that the time for acting on it might very probably come. I think the time has come now. I wish it were a better time. I wish that we were in a better condition. The action of the army against the rebels has not been quite what I should have best liked. But they have been driven out of Maryland, and Pennsylvania is no longer in danger of invasion. When the rebel army was at Frederick, I determined, as soon as it should be driven out of Maryland, to issue a Proclamation of Emancipation such as I thought most likely to be useful. I said nothing to any one; but I made the promise to myself, and (hesitating a little)—to my Maker. The rebel army is now driven out, and I am going to fulfil that promise. I have got you together to hear what I have written down."

A Mixed Reception for Emancipation

Abraham Lincoln, preliminary Emancipation Proclamation, September 22, 1862:

That on the first day of January in the year of our Lord, one thousand eight hundred and sixty-three, all persons held as slaves within any state, or designated part of a state, the people whereof shall then be in rebellion against the United States shall be then, thenceforward, and forever free; and the executive government of the United States, including the military and naval authority thereof, will recognize and maintain the freedom of such persons, and will do no act or acts to repress such persons, or any of them, in any efforts they may make for their actual freedom.

God bless you for *a good deed!*

>   —*Theodore Tilton to Abraham Lincoln, reacting to announcement of the Emancipation Proclamation, September 22, 1862*

We shout for joy that we live to record this righteous decree.

>   —*Frederick Douglass, reacting to announcement of the Emancipation Proclamation, September 22, 1862*

A large majority can see no reason why *they* should be shot for the benefit of niggers and Abolitionists.

>   —*An Ohio editor, reacting to announcement of the Emancipation Proclamation, September 22, 1862*

We shall not stop now to discuss the character and tendency of this measure. Both are manifest. The one is as unwarrantable as the other is mischievous. The measure is wholly unauthorized and wholly pernicious.

>   —*The Louisville* Journal, *reacting to announcement of the Emancipation Proclamation, September 22, 1862*

It is very doubtful whether I shall remain in the service after the rebels have left this vicinity. The Presdt's late Proclamation . . . [makes it] almost impossible for me to retain my commission & self respect at the same time. I cannot make up my mind to fight for such an accursed doctrine as that of a servile insurrection—it is too infamous.

—Gen. George B. McClellan to his wife Mary Ellen,
September 25, 1862, Sharpsburg, Maryland

Civil Liberties in Civil War

Whereas . . . disloyal persons are not adequately restrained by the ordinary processes of law from . . . giving aid and comfort in various ways to the insurrection . . . the Writ of Habeas Corpus is suspended in respect to all persons arrested, or who are now, or hereafter during the rebellion shall be, imprisoned in any fort, camp, arsenal, military prison, or other place of confinement by any military authority or by the sentence of any Court Martial or Military Commission.

—Abraham Lincoln, September 24, 1862

(Ironically, Lincoln issued this proclamation—official validation of what historian Mark E. Neely, Jr., called "the low tide for liberty" in America—just two days after issuing his preliminary Emancipation Proclamation. It earned Lincoln from many detractors the label of tyrant, but the President insisted that had he instead preserved the right of habeas corpus, the country itself would have been destroyed.)

. . .

Peter W. Alexander ("A"), writing in the Mobile *Daily Advertiser* from the Confederate lines in Maryland, October 4, 1862:

Do you wonder, then, that there should have been stragglers from the army? That brave and true men should have fallen out of line from sheer exhaustion, or in their efforts to obtain a mouthful to eat along the roadside? Or that many seasoned veterans should have succumbed to disease and been forced back to the hospital? I look to hear a great outcry raised against the stragglers. Already lazy cavalry men and dainty staff officers, who are mounted and can forage the country for something to eat, are condemning the weary private, who, notwithstanding his body may be covered with dust and perspiration and his feet with stonebruises, is expected to trudge along under his knapsack and cartridge belt on empty stomach and never to turn aside for a morsel of food to sustain his sinking limbs. . . . He suffers and toils and fights for you, too, brave, true-hearted women of the South. Will you not clothe his nakedness then? Will you not put shoes and stockings on his feet? Is it not enough that he has written down his patriotism in crimson characters along the battle-road from the Rappahannock to the Potomac, and must his bleeding feet also impress their mark of fidelity upon the snows of the coming winter? I know what your answer will be. God has spoken through the women of the

---

. . . **September 23.** Sioux uprising ends with their defeat at Battle of Wood Lake, Minnesota . . . **September 24.** Lincoln issues new order suspending writ of *habeas corpus* nationwide . . . **October 3–4.** Union wins Battle of Corinth, Mississippi . . . .

South, and they are his holy oracles in this day of trial and tribulation.

Midshipman James M. Morgan, C.S.A., aboard the S. S. *Herald* off Charleston harbor, October 9, 1862:

We made another attempt to get through the blockade. All lights were out except the one in the covered binnacle protecting the compass. Not a word was spoken save by the pilot, who gave his orders in whispers. The captain had no desire to be taken prisoner, as he had been proclaimed a pirate by the Federal government. He was convinced that the great danger in running the blockade was in his own engine room, so he seated himself there with a revolver on the ladder leading down to it and politely informed the engineer that if the engine stopped clear of the fleet, he, the engineer, would be a dead man.

(The *Herald* made it to Bermuda. Still, by 1862, an estimated one out of every seven vessels leaving Southern ports was captured by Union blockaders—an astounding record, considering that the Federal navy was guarding more than 3,500 miles of coastline.)

Abraham Lincoln to George B. McClellan, October 25, 1862:

I have just read your despatch about sore tongued and fatiegued [*sic*] horses. Will you pardon me for asking

... **October 8.** Union wins Battle of Perryville, Kentucky ....

what the horses of your army have done since the battle of Antietam that fatigue anything?

(McClellan replied to this famous, caustic telegraph message with an elaborate defense of his long month of military inactivity, concluding, "If any instance can be found where overworked cavalry has performed more labor than mine . . . I am not aware of it." Not to be outdone, Lincoln had the final word: "Will not a movement of our army be a relief to the cavalry?")

Capt. John William De Forest, 12th Connecticut Volunteers, recalling his first exposure to enemy fire, near Thibodeaux, Louisiana, October 26, 1862:

I believed that the eyes of all my soldiers were upon me (whereas they were probably looking only for the enemy); and so, for reason's sake and example's sake, I kept my head steadfast. It cost me no great effort. I had no nervous inclination to duck, no involuntary twitching or trembling; I was not aware of any painful quickening of the pulse; in short, I was not frightened. I thought to myself, it is very possible that they will hit me, but I hope not, and I think not. It seemed to me the most natural thing in the world that others should be killed, and that I should not. . . . We were just entering a large open field, dotted by a few trees and thorn-bushes, with a swamp forest on the right and the levee of the bayou on the left, when the rebels gave us their musketry. It was not a volley, but a file fire—it was a long rattle like that which a boy makes in running with a stick along a picket-fence, only vastly louder; and at the same time the sharp, quick *whit whit* of bullets chippered close to our ears. In the field little puffs of dust jumped up here and there; on the other side of it a long, low blue roll of smoke curled upward; to the right of it the gray smoke of the artillery arose in a thin cloud; but no other vestige of the enemy was visible.

June McVeigh to President Jefferson Davis, received November 18, 1862:

I am a Widow upward of seventy years of age a cripple for life my home and property distroyed and dispoiled by the inhuman enemy and left entirely without resources of any kind and no one in the world to look to for support . . . but my son (or the cold charities of the public) with the rigours of winter staring me in the face.

(The widow McVeigh's plea that her son be discharged to help support her at home—along with many others like it that season—was referred to the Confederate secretary of war. There is no record of a reply.)

Robert Stiles, Richmond Howitzers, describing the evacuation of civilians from Fredericksburg, Virginia, on the eve of battle, November 27, 1862:

There were women carrying a baby in one arm, and its bottle, its clothes, and its covering in the other. Some

. . . **November 7.** Lincoln removes McClellan, names Gen. Ambrose E. Burnside commander of Army of Potomac . . . .

had a Bible and a toothbrush in one hand, a picked chicken and a bag of flour in the other. Most of them had to cross a creek swollen with winter rains, and deadly cold with winter ice and snow. We took the battery horses down and ferried them over, taking one child in front and two behind, and sometimes a woman or a girl in either side with her feet in the stirrups, holding on by our shoulders. Where they were going we could not tell, and I doubt if they could.

Abraham Lincoln, annual message to Congress, December 1, 1862:

We cannot escape history. We of this Congress and this administration, will be remembered in spite of ourselves. No personal significance, or insignificance, can spare one or another of us. The fiery trial through which we pass, will light us down, in honor or dishonor, to the latest generation. We *say* we are for the Union. The world will not forget that we say this. We know how to save the Union. The world knows we do know how to save it. We—even *we here*—hold the power, and bear the responsibility. In *giving* freedom to the *slave*, we *assure* freedom to the *free*—honorable alike in what we give, and what we preserve. We shall nobly save, or meanly lose, the last best, hope of earth.

───────────────────────────────────

... **December 1.** Lincoln proposes compensated emancipation in Union slave states; plan for colonizing freedmen, in "We cannot escape history" annual message to Congress ....

(The equivalent of today's State of the Union messages—
although it was not read aloud by the President—this eloquent appeal to keep alive the promise of the Emancipation
Proclamation came just one month before The Emancipation
was scheduled to take effect.)

Cpl. Columbus H. Gray, 29th Arkansas Infantry, to his father,
reporting the death of his brother, Sgt. "Ad" Gray, at the
Battle of Prairie Grove, Arkansas, December 7, 1862:

Now I expect you want to know wat I did with my
Brothers boddy. I am sorry to say that I had to leave him
on the field. Just at night I went to him. Oh my God he
looked so pale and bad and there was a tear in one of his
eyes. I throwed my armed around him and hollowed to
some of the boys to come help me carry him off the field
and they would not come. . . . So I laid him on his back
and stritened him out and had to leave him. We left the
field that knight and so did the Federals. They say that
their killed and wounded was eight to our one. I can tell
you we showed them shame.

A "Terrible Grandeur"

The air became thick with the murky clouds. The earth
shook beneath the terrific explosions of the shells, which
went howling over the river, crashing into the houses,
battering down walls, splintering doors, ripping up
floors. Sixty solid shot and shells a minute were thrown,
and the bombardment was kept up till nine thousand

were fired. No hot shot were used, but the explosions set fire to a block of houses, which added terrible grandeur to the scene.

—Correspondent for the Boston Journal,
December 12, 1862

(Union forces bombarded the town of Fredericksburg before attacking across the Rappahannock River, driving residents of the Virginia town into nearby woods for safety.)

A Fondness for War

It is well that war is so terrible; we should grow too fond of it.

—Gen. Robert E. Lee, observing the Union advance at
Fredericksburg, December 13, 1862

I wish these people would go away and let us alone.

—Also attributed to Lee at Fredericksburg

Peter W. Alexander ("A"), writing in the Mobile *Daily Advertiser*, December 13, 1862:

The enemy made a desperate attempt to gain these heights. Assault upon assault was made, each time with fresh columns and increased numbers. They never succeeded, however, in getting nearer than seventy or eighty yards to the stone wall, from which the brave Georgians and Carolinians saluted them with a fire that no mere human force could face and yet live. Our men did not pull a trigger until they got within easy range, and then taking deliberate aim, they poured volley after volley right into their faces . . . repulsed the foe with a slaughter that is without a parallel in this war. I went over the ground this morning, and the remaining dead, after two-thirds of them had been removed, lay twice as thick as upon any other battlefield I have ever seen.

(The hopeless Union assault on impregnable Confederate positions atop Marye's Heights turned the Battle of Fredericksburg, on December 13, 1862, into the biggest federal disaster of the war. The Union lost more than 12,000 men before retreating.)

Facing "Hell" on Marye's Heights

The Yankees had essayed a task which no army . . . could have accomplished. To have driven our men from their position and to have taken it, was a work compared with which the storming of Gibraltar would be as child's play.

—Frank Moore, Southern journalist, commenting on the
Union assault at Fredericksburg, December 13, 1862

It can hardly be in human nature for men to show more valor, or Generals to manifest less judgement, than were perceptible on our side that day.

—Correspondent for the Cincinnati Daily Commercial, December 13, 1862

It was a great slaughter pen. . . . [We] might as well have tried to take hell.

—A Union soldier describing the attack on Marye's Heights, Fredericksburg, December 13, 1862

(As historian E. B. Long summarized the ill-conceived, ill-fated Union charge toward the heavily entrenched stone wall atop Marye's Heights: "The heroism was there, but not the strategy.")

Gen. Darius N. Couch, U.S.A., describing the charge up Marye's Heights, Battle of Fredericksburg, December 13, 1862:

I had never before seen fighting like that—nothing approaching it in terrible uproar and destruction. . . . As they charged, the artillery fire would break their formation and they would get mixed. Then they would close up, go forward, receive the withering infantry fire, and . . . fight as best they could. And then the next brigade, coming up in succession would do its duty, and melt like snow coming down on the warm ground.

Gen. James Longstreet, C.S.A., December 13, 1862:

The Federals had fallen like the steady dripping of rain from the eaves of a house.

A Union soldier writing home after the Battle of Fredericksburg:

I saw one man with gun in hand, walking with a firm step and a cheerful countenance, having been struck by a piece of shell in the forehead, laying bare the brain so I could see every pulsation.

. . .

Gen. Ulysses S. Grant, General Order No. 11, Headquarters, Dept. of Tennessee, December 17, 1862:

The Jews, as a class violating every regulation of trade established by the Treasury Department and also department orders, are hereby expelled from the department within twenty-four hours from the receipt of this order. Post commanders will see that all of this class of people be furnished passes and required to leave, and any one returning after such notification will be arrested and held in confinement until an opportunity occurs of sending them out as prisoners unless furnished with a permit from headquarters.

(Jews loyal to the Union quickly lodged protests at the White House against Grant's notorious order, whereupon Lincoln instructed his general-in-chief to order it rescinded on January 4. "I don't like to see a class or nationality condemned on account of a few sinners," Lincoln told a Jewish delegation a few days later.)

Pvt. Constantine A. Hege to his "dearly beloved parents," December 18, 1862, near Fredericksburg, Virginia:

The human suffering, the loss of life and above all the loss of many a precious soul that is caused by war— would to God this war might end with the close of the year and we could all enjoy the blessing of a comfortable house and home one time more. I never knew how to value home until I came in the army.

1863

WHAT WAS LEFT of the fractured American Union would perhaps never experience an Independence Day as glorious as the one it celebrated on July 4, 1863.

Only a day before, the Confederacy had ascended—and then toppled—from its "high water mark" at Gettysburg, the greatest battle of the entire war. And then, on the Fourth itself, Vicksburg, under relentless bombardment since May, finally surrendered to Gen. Ulysses S. Grant. With twin victories in both the east and the west, Northerners had every reason to believe that the rebellion was at last losing steam.

They were soon proven wrong.

Although Lee had lost his "right arm" when "Stonewall" Jackson fell at the otherwise triumphant Battle of Chancellorsville in May, his troops—ill-clothed and ill-equipped though they were—fought on bravely. Federal forces continued to amass battlefield victories—at Port Hudson, Knoxville, and Chattanooga—but Lee's army was no nearer capitulating than they had been after losing at Antietam the year before.

Human endurance at home remained extraordinarily strong. In Vicksburg, women were driven from their homes into caves to escape Union shelling. Throughout the South, women went without clothing, and children without food. Southern and Northern families alike sacrificed fathers, husbands, and sons—or welcomed home survivors hobbled by shattered limbs and indelible nightmares.

Soldiers on both sides continued to witness unimaginable horrors on the battlefield—and record their impressions in letters and diaries. But in 1863 a new force entered the fray—so-called "colored" troops. Relegated at first to menial duty in Union camps, black soldiers achieved glory with their heroic, fateful charge against Battery Wagner on July 18. The assault failed, but the federal army emerged with a strong, new "sable arm"—men fighting not merely to preserve their Union or their property, but to earn their own freedom.

Not that either government—Lincoln's in the North or Davis's in the South—enjoyed unqualified support. In Richmond, racked by deprivation, a group of angry, starving women rampaged through the streets and looted stores; the "Bread Riots" were not calmed until Jefferson Davis himself appeared on the scene to appeal for peace. In New York a few months later, mobs protesting the Union's first draft laws rioted even more ferociously, killing innocent black bystanders—whom they blamed for the war—and setting fire to an orphan asylum for black children. It took federal troops to quiet this disturbance, the worst example of civil unrest in all American history—save for the Civil War itself.

Americans on both sides were understandably tiring of bloodshed and sacrifice. But on November 19, Lincoln managed to consecrate both a soldiers' cemetery and the cause for which its silent occupants had died when he reached his rhetorical zenith at Gettysburg. Lincoln proclaimed a "new birth of freedom" in his most famous address—adding poetry to the dry, legalistic prose of his final Emancipation Proclamation, which he signed on New Year's Day. "The world will little note nor long remember what we say here," Lincoln insisted at Gettysburg. It was, perhaps, the most erroneous prediction he ever made.

Abraham Lincoln, final Emancipation Proclamation, January 1, 1863:

I do order and declare that all persons held as slaves within said designated States, and parts of States, are, and henceforward, shall be, free; and that the Executive government of the United States, including the military and naval authorities thereof, will recognize and maintain the freedom of said persons. . . . And upon this act, sincerely believed to be an act of justice, warranted by the Constitution, upon military necessity, I invoke the considerate judgement of mankind, and the gracious favor of Almighty God.

(One writer complained years later that Lincoln's greatest act boasted "all the moral grandeur of a bill of lading." But Lincoln preferred a sound legal document that could withstand later court challenges to a flowery statement issued "from the bosom of philanthropy." He surely knew that merely signing the document was itself historic when he stated: "If my name ever goes into history, it will be because of this act.")

Harriet Beecher Stowe, writing in the *Atlantic Monthly,* January 1863:

Mark our words! If we succeed, the children of these very men who are now fighting us will rise up to call us blessed. Just as surely as there is a God who governs the world, so surely all the laws of national prosperity follow in the train of equity; and if we succeed, we shall have delivered the children's children of our misguided brethren from the wages of sin, which is always and everywhere death.

Varina Howell Davis, wife of the Confederate president, remembering the announcement of the Emancipation Proclamation, January 1, 1863:

The effect of the Emancipation Proclamation on the people of the South was unmistakable. It roused them to a determination to resist to the uttermost a power that respected neither the rights of property nor constitutional guarantees. . . . The condition of our servants began to be unsettled, and it was said there were clubs of disaffected colored men in Richmond, generally presided over by a white man, who were furnished with two thousand dollars for each servant who ran off from our service.

"Agnes" to Mrs. Roger A. Pryor, January 7, 1863, Richmond, Virginia:

Do you realize that we shall soon be without a stitch of clothes? There is not a bonnet for sale in Richmond. Some of the girls smuggle them, which I for one consider in the worst possible taste, to say the least. We have no right at this time to dress better than our neighbors, and besides, the soldiers need every cent of our money. Do you remember in Washington my pearl-gray silk bonnet, trimmed inside with lilies of the valley? I have ripped it up, washed and ironed it, dyed the lilies blue (they are bluebells now), and it is very becoming. . . . It seems rather volatile to discuss such things while our dear country is in such peril. Heaven knows I would costume myself in coffee-bags if that would help, but having no coffee, where could I get the bags?

("Agnes"—probably the wife of a federal official who went south after secession—preferred to be known to history only by her given name, "being a lady of the old school," according to the recipient of this letter.)

. . . **January 4.** Lincoln rescinds Gen. Grant's order banning "Jews as a class" from federal lines . . . .

Col. Marcus Spiegel, 67th Ohio Volunteers, to his wife,
Caroline, January 25, 1863:

I am sick of the war. . . . I do not fight or want to fight
for Lincoln's Negro proclamation one day longer.

(Spiegel, the highest-ranking Jewish officer in the Union
army, fought on anyway, and soon had a change of heart.
Horrified by what he saw of slavery firsthand as he fought
through Louisiana, he went so far as to declare himself "a
strong abolitionist" shortly before being killed in action in
January 1864.)

A private in the 22nd Massachusetts Infantry, undergoing
treatment at a Union army field hospital, ca. 1863:

A large hole was dug in the yard, about the size of a
small cellar, and into this the legs and arms were thrown
as they were lopped off by the surgeons, with a coolness
that would be a terror to persons unaccustomed to the
sight of military surgery after a battle. The day was hot
and sultry, and the odor of the ether used in the operations and the effluvia from the receptacle of mangled
limbs, was sickening in the extreme. Flies came down
upon us in clouds, torturing us.

(No one knows how many emergency amputations were performed in field hospitals during the Civil War, but by one
often-quoted account, the largest item in one Southern state's
postwar budget was allocated for prostheses for Confederate
veterans. Only the best-stocked wartime hospitals boasted ad-

equate supplies of ether; countless amputations were performed without any anesthetic.)

Henry E. Schafer, musician with the 103rd Illinois, in a letter to his wife, January 18, 1863:

In our camps wickedness prevails to almost unlimited extent. It looks to me as though some men try to see how depraved they can be. Gambling, Card Playing, Profanity, Sabbath Breaking &c are among the many vices practiced by many of the men. . . . It sometimes seems to me that the Almighty would never bless the efforts of our army to put down this rebellion while it is so depraved.

William Swinton, the New York *Times*, recalling Burnside's march across the Rappahannock River, Virginia, January 22, 1863:

The bottom had dropped out of the entire region. Mud is no name by which to describe the sticky, miry, pitchy, unfathomable, and unexplorable semifluid beds of stuff which filled and overflowed the roads, every one of which was transformed into an abysmal slough of despond. The army was literally stuck in the mud . . . as absolutely helpless as though the rebel army had come upon them when asleep and bound them hand and foot. . . . Horses and mules dropped down dead, exhausted with the effort to move their loads through the hideous medium . . . many of them buried in the liquid muck.

. . . **January 19–23.** Union army bogs down in "Mud March" . . . .

Mary Cooper to her husband, Edward Cooper, C.S.A., ca. February 1, 1863:

I would not have you do anything wrong for the world; but before God, Edward, unless you come home we must die! Last night I was aroused by little Eddie's crying. I called and said "What's the matter, Eddie?" and he said, "Oh, mamma, I'm so hungry." And Lucy, Edward, your darling Lucy, she never complains, but she is growing thinner and thinner every day.

(Unable to obtain a furlough, Cooper returned home without leave. At his wife's urging, he went back to his regiment, where he was court-martialed for desertion. Gen. Lee intervened to pardon him, and Cooper returned to active service—only to be killed in action.)

Frederick Douglass, address in New York City, February 6, 1863:

It is again objected to this Proclamation that it is only an ink and paper proclamation. I admit it. The objector might go a step further, and assert that there was a time when this Proclamation was only a thought, a sentiment, an idea—a hope of some radical Abolitionist—for such it truly was. But what of it? The world has never advanced a single inch in the right direction, when the movement could not be traced to some such small beginning. . . . The freedom of the American colonies dates from no

. . . **January 26.** Lincoln names Gen. Joseph Hooker to replace Burnside as commander of Army of Potomac . . . .

particular battle during the war. No man can tell upon what particular day we won our national independence. But the birth of freedom is fixed on the day of the going forth of the Declaration of Independence. In like manner aftercoming generations will celebrate the first of January as the day which brought liberty and manhood to the American slaves. How shall this be done? I answer: That the paper Proclamation must now be made iron, lead and fire, by the prompt employment of the negro's arm in this contest. I hold that the Proclamation, good as it is, will be worthless—a miserable mockery—unless the nation shall so far conquer its prejudice as to welcome into the army full-grown black men to help fight the battles of the Republic.

John B. Jones, clerk to President Davis, February 11, 1863, Richmond:

Some idea may be formed of the scarcity of food in this city from the fact that, while my youngest daughter was in the kitchen to-day, a young rat came out of its hole and seemed to beg for something to eat; she held out some bread, which it ate from her hand, and seemed grateful. Several others soon appeared, and were as tame as kittens. Perhaps we shall have to eat them!

Pvt. Richard H. Puffer, 8th Illinois Infantry, February 12, 1863, Memphis, Tennessee:

I have slept on the soft side of a board, in the mud, and every other place that was lousey and dirty; I have drank out of goose ponds, horse tracks, etc., for the last eighteen months, all for the poor nigger; and I have yet to see the first one that I think has been benefitted by it.

Walt Whitman, writing in the New York *Times*, February 26, 1863:

Every form of wound, (the mere sight of some of them having been known to make a tolerably hardy visitor faint away,) every kind of malady, like a long procession, with typhoid fever and diarrhoea at the head as leaders, are here in steady motion. The soldier's hospital! How many sleepless nights, how many woman's tears, how many long and aching hours and days of suspense, from every one of the Middle, Eastern and Western States have concentrated here!

(After traveling to Washington to find his wounded brother, Whitman became a self-described "missionary" to the city's military hospitals, ministering to the maimed, and visiting by war's end—according to his own estimate—80,000–100,000 soldiers.)

Two Views of Guerilla War

The exploits of Captain Mosby would furnish material for a volume which would resemble rather a romance. . . . It is only necessary to glance at the Captain to understand that he was cut out for a partisan leader.

His figure is slight, muscular, supple and vigorous; his eye is keen, penetrating, ever on the alert; he wears his sabre and pistol with the air of a man who sleeps with them buckled around his waist; and handles them habitually, almost unconsciously. The Captain is a determined man in a charge, dangerous on a scout, hard to outwit, and prone to "turn up" suddenly when he is least expected, and bang away with pistol and carbine. . . . As the sharpshooters advanced, led on gallantly by the Captain, who galloped about cheering his imaginary squadron, the enemy were seized with a sudden panic, wavered, and gave way, thus presenting the comic and highly interesting spectacle of an entire Yankee brigade retiring before a party of eight or ten sharpshooters!

> —Lt. John Esten Cooke, C.S.A., describing one of John
> Singleton Mosby's raids near Warrenton, Virginia, ca.
> March 1863

No sooner had our men surrendered, the Rebels instantly commenced robbing the train and murdering their prisoners, even the wounded. Here is the scene or a sample of it—ten minutes after. Among the wounded officers in the ambulances were one, a lieutenant of regulars, and another, of higher rank. These two were dragged out on the ground on their backs and were now surrounded by the guerrillas, a demoniac crowd, each member of which was stabbing them in different parts of their bodies. One of the officers had his feet pinned firmly to the ground by bayonets stuck through them and thrust into the ground. . . . Multiply the above by scores, aye hundreds . . . light it with every lurid passion—the wolf's, the lion's lapping thirst for blood; the passionate, boiling volcanoes of human revenge for comrades, brothers slain . . . and in the human heart everywhere, black, worse embers—and you have an inkling of the war.

—*Walt Whitman, describing one of Mosby's raids near Upperton, Virginia, date unknown*

John Tallman, company musician, 76th Illinois Volunteer Infantry, to his sister, Amanda, March 1, 1863, Lafayette, Tennessee:

You made a good deal of fun of my washing in a mud pudle, but you had better blieve I can make my clothes look real nice. I put them on to iron them and starch them with dirt, so I guess you had better not come down here, for I can beat you a washing; and cook—why you are no whare. I can fry meat, make coffee, boil potatoes when we have any, build fire, fetch water—in fact, do a right smart sprinkling of things. So when I come home I will learn you how to cook if you want me to, and I am comeing home pretty soon, for I have only thirty months more to stay.

(Drummer boy Tallman did not live to instruct his sister in the domestic arts. Regimental records show he died on March 19, 1865, three weeks before the war ended.)

. . .

Cpl. James Henry Gooding, 54th Massachusetts Volunteer
Infantry, March 3, 1863:

Our people must know that if they are ever to attain to
any position in the eyes of the civilized world, they must
forgo comfort, home, fear, and above all, superstition,
and fight for it; make up their minds to become something more than hewers of wood and drawers of water all
their lives. Consider that on this continent, at least, their
race and name will be totally obliterated unless they put
forth some effort now to save themselves.

(Reminiscences by black soldiers of the Civil War are ex-
tremely rare. A major exception was Corporal Gooding who,
for a full year, contributed a weekly letter to the New Bedford
Mercury, from the first of which this concluding paragraph is
excerpted. The author was a member of the most fabled
"colored" regiment of the war, the unit destined to achieve
glory at Battery Wagner later that year.)

Howell Cobb, 1863:

The day you make soldiers of them is the beginning of
the end of the revolution. If slaves will make good soldiers, our whole theory of slavery is wrong.

(Cobb, a onetime Congressman and Governor of Georgia,
chaired the 1861 Montgomery convention at which the Confederacy was organized, and later became Speaker of the
Provisional Congress and a Confederate general. Despite his
warnings, some 200,000 black soldiers went on to serve in the

Union Army, fighting in 449 engagements, and suffering 35% more casualties than their white counterparts.)

Charles G. Halpine of New York, writing under the pseudonym "Private Miles O'Reilly," 1863:

> *Some tell us 'tis a burnin shame*
> *To make the naygers fight;*
> *An that the thrade of bein' kilt*
> *Belongs but to the white;*
> *But as for me, upon my soul!*
> *So liberal are we here,*
> *I'll let Sambo be murthered instead of myself*
> *On every day of the year.*

John B. Jones, clerk to President Davis, diary entry, March 13, 1863, Richmond:

To-day a great calamity occurred in this city. In a large room of one of the government laboratories an explosion took place, killing instantly five or six persons, and wounding, it is feared fatally, some thirty others. Most of them were little indigent girls!

(A so-called "friction primer" at the Confederate Ordnance Laboratory accidentally ignited, causing the explosion. The final toll was sixty-nine dead or injured, sixty-two of whom were women. Jones, however, did not retain his sympathy for women compelled to work during the war. When a project was launched the following year to introduce "lady clerks" into his own bureau, he complained that their places should instead be filled by "poor refugees, who have suffered most.")

Gen. James A. Garfield, U.S.A., to his wife Lucretia, April 1, 1863, Murfreesboro, Tennessee:

There is such a mystery about life in any form that the contemplation of it always fills me with awe. But of incipient life, of life that is to be, with all the grand and fearful possibilities which may attend it, I have no words to tell you what my thoughts were. And then the thought that is my life, a life which I may never see, that there may be a period of oblivion between the sunset of my own and the morning of that new life. Should this be true that little life will be so strange and singular as one in its history. It is impossible for me to tell you how overwhelming and deep an interest I feel in the future of that precious hope. I beg you to be happy and cheerful during all the awfully mysterious days through which you will live till the consummation.

(Gen. Garfield lived not only to see the birth of his son, Harry, on October 11, but to win election to the presidency in 1880.)

John B. Jones, clerk to President Davis, describing the bread riot in Richmond, April 2, 1863:

This morning early a few hundred women and boys met as by concert in the Capitol Square, saying they were hungry, and must have food. The number continued to swell until there were more than a thousand . . . [and] they marched through Cary Street, and entered diverse stores of the speculators, which they proceeded to empty of their contents. They impressed all the carts and drays in the street, which were speedily laden with meal, flour, shoes . . . turned into Main Street . . . broke in the plate-glass windows, demanding silks, jewelry, etc. . . . About this time the President appeared . . . urged them to return to their homes, so that the bayonets there menacing them might be sent against the common enemy. He told them that such acts would bring *famine* upon them . . . said he was willing to share his last loaf with the suffering people . . . trusted we would all bear our privations with fortitude.

(Davis's pleas failed to disperse the angry, starving crowd. Only when an armed military force gave the rioters five minutes to disperse did the riot finally end. It was the worst civilian disturbance to roil the Confederacy during the war.)

Pvt. James Hammer, C. S. A., 21st Tennessee Cavalry, to his mother, April 11, 1863, from camp near Franklin, Tennessee:

Tell Mr. Alford I am getting tired of the army, and would like to help him fish this summer, but fear I will have other fish to fry.

Pvt. Wiley Britton, 6th Kansas Cavalry, April 23, 1863, near
Fort Gibson, Indian Territory:

A spy was caught to-day near camp, dressed in a
woman's suit. He is a young fellow with light hair, a fair
complexion, of a rather prepossessing appearance, and
I should think not over sixteen years of age. When I saw
him in the Provost-Marshal's tent he seemed to be badly
frightened, in fact almost frightened out of his wits. . . . It
was by the merest accident that he was detected. When
several of our Indian soldiers first saw him . . . [they]
noticed that his movements were peculiar, and not like
those of a woman, and when they came towards him, he
started to run. . . . If I were going as a spy into the
enemy's camp, to dress in a woman's suit would be about
the last method I should think of adopting, even if I had
as marked feminine features as some young men, which
I have not.

Rev. A. M. Stewart, Union chaplain, remembering the sound
of the Rebel yell at Chancellorsville, May 2, 1863:

This strange, curious, unearthly sound seems peculiar
to Johnny Reb. The nearest transfer into print may be
"Ki-*yi*—ki-*yi*—ki-*yi*," with a vigorous screech on the *"yi."*
This, uttered in the darkness of night, amid the crash of
firearms, and by a flushed and determined enemy, who,

... **April 16.** Union fleet under Adm. David D. Porter bursts through Confederate
batteries at Vicksburg, Mississippi . . . **May 1.** Grant captures Port Gibson, Mississippi
. . . **May 1–4.** Confederates win Battle of Chancellorsville, Virginia . . . .

at the same time, must have been thirty to our one, had, it must be confessed, somewhat of terror connected therewith.

Lt. J. F. J. Caldwell, C.S.A., recalling the "wild and fierce" night fighting at Chancellorsville, Virginia, May 2, 1863:

Night engagements are always dreadful, but this was the worst I ever knew. To see your danger is bad enough; but to hear shell whizzing and bursting over you, to hear shrapnel and iron fragments slapping the trees and cracking off limbs, and not know from whence death comes to you, is trying beyond all things. And here it looked so incongruous—*below*, rage, thunder, shout, shriek, slaughter; *above*, soft, silent, moonlight and peace.

The Death of Jackson

Maj. Henry Kyd Douglas, Jackson's staff officer, describing the accidental shooting of the Confederate general at Chancellorsville, Virginia, May 2, 1863:

Suddenly from the rear came a cry of "Yankee Cavalry!" and a sharp volley [from Confederate pickets] rang out on the night air and sent death among its friends. General Jackson was shot through the left arm below the shoulder, and in the left wrist. . . . "Little Sorrel" [Jackson's horse] became frantic with fright, rushed first toward the enemy, then, being turned by the General with his wounded hand, broke again to the rear.

The General was struck in the face by a hanging limb, his cap was knocked from his head. . . . Others of the party were killed or wounded, and verily, in the language of General Sherman, "war was hell" that night.

(Jackson developed pneumonia and died eight days later.)

Maj. Henry Kyd Douglas, Jackson's staff officer, recalling his chief's death, May 10, 1863:

It is said that a semi-lunatic was walking on the lawn of an asylum near Baltimore when someone announced to him the death of Stonewall Jackson. At the news he was dazed, disturbed, and his feeble mind seemed to be groping in the dark for some explanation for such a calamity. Deep sadness settled upon his face. Then suddenly a light broke over it and lifting his head and looking up into the sky he explained, "Oh, what a battle must have been raging in Heaven, when the Archangel of the Lord needed the services of Stonewall Jackson!"

Chancellorsville

Gen. Abner Doubleday, later credited by some with inventing baseball, remembering the Union retreat at Chancellorsville, May 3, 1863:

The exhausted troops put their caps on their bayonets, waved them aloft, and with loud cheers charged on the rebels and drove them out once more; but sixty guns opened upon them at close range with terrible effect; the promised reinforcements did not come; they were surrounded with ever increasing enemies, and forced to give up everything and retreat. . . . Had they been disposed to follow up the retreat closely they would have been unable to do so, for now a new and terrible barrier intervened; the woods on each side of the Plank Road had been set on fire by the artillery and the wounded and dying were burning in the flames without a possibility of rescuing them. Let us draw a veil over this scene, for it is pitiful to dwell upon it.

Col. Charles Marshall, military secretary to Gen. Lee, recalling Lee's ride along the front at the Battle of Chancellorsville, May 3, 1863:

His presence was the signal for one of those uncontrollable outbursts of enthusiasm which none can appreciate who have not witnessed them. The fierce soldiers, with their faces blackened with the smoke of battle, the wounded crawling with feeble limbs from the fury of the devouring flames, all seemed possessed with a common impulse. One long, unbroken cheer, in which the feeble cry of those who lay helpless on the earth blended with the strong voices of those who still fought, rose high above the roar of battle and hailed the presence of the victorious chief . . . and as I looked upon him . . . I thought that it must have been from some such scene that men in ancient days ascended to the dignity of gods.

Pvt. John Casler, C. S. A., describing the aftermath of the
Battle of Chancellorsville, May 4, 1863:

The dead and badly wounded from both sides were
lying where they fell. The woods, taking fire that night
from the shells, burnt rapidly and roasted the wounded
men alive. As we went to bury them we could see where
they had tried to keep the fire from them by scratching
the leaves away as far as they could reach. But it availed
not; they were burnt to a crisp. The only way we could
tell to which army they belonged was by turning them
over and examining their clothing where they lay close
to the ground.

Anguish After Chancellorsville

Abraham Lincoln, on hearing the news of the Union defeat at
Chancellorsville, May 4, 1863:

My God! My God! What will the country say? What will
the country say?

Jefferson Davis on the death of "Stonewall" Jackson, May 10,
1863:

Our loss was much less in killed and wounded than
that of the enemy, but of the number was one, a host in
himself, Lieutenant General Jackson . . . war has seldom
shown an equal.

. . . **May 10.** Stonewall Jackson, shot accidentally by his own men at Chancellorsville,
dies of complications from wound . . . .

Robert E. Lee on the death of "Stonewall" Jackson, May 10, 1863:

I have lost my right arm.

(The Union lost more than 11,000 men at Chancellorsville—but in the final analysis, the Confederacy probably suffered a far greater loss with the death of Jackson, shot by his own pickets, who mistook him for the enemy.)

. . .

Special correspondent for the Augusta *Daily Constitutionalist,* ca. May 17, 1863:

I told you we would stay until starved out. Well, rats are a luxury. Small fishes sell at twenty dollars. Chickens at ten dollars each. Corn meal has sold at one hundred and sixty dollars per bushel. Mule meat has sold readily at two dollars per pound, in market, and I eat it once a week. The soldiers have had only one meal a day for ten days, and then one man does not get what a child should have.

(After a protracted siege that forced many residents into caves to escape Union shells, Vicksburg surrendered to the Union on July 4, 1863—unleashing frenzied celebrations in the North, and unfettered gloom in the South. But the capture undoubtedly brought relief to the citizens who had lived in such degrading conditions for so long.)

. . . **May 14.** Grant captures Jackson, Mississippi . . . **May 16–17.** Confederate defenses outside Vicksburg crumble . . . .

Mary Ann Loughborough, late May 1863, from her 1864 memoir, *My Cave Life in Vicksburg:*

The cave we inhabited was about five squares from the levee. A great many had been made in a hill immediately beyond us; and near us; and near this hill we could see most of the shells fall. Caves were the fashion—the rage—over besieged Vicksburg. Negroes, who understood their business, hired themselves out to dig them, at from thirty to fifty dollars, according to the size. . . . So great was the demand for cave workmen that a new branch of industry sprang up and became popular. . . . Even the very animals seemed to share the general fear of a sudden and frightful death. The dogs would be seen in the midst of the noise to gallop up the street, and then to return, as if fear had maddened them. On hearing the descent of a shell, they would dart aside—then, as it exploded, sit down and howl in the most pitiful manner. The horses, belonging to the officers, and fastened to the trees near the tents, would frequently strain the halter to its full length, rearing high in the air, with a loud snort of terror, as a shell would explode near. I could hear them in the night cry out in the midst of the uproar, ending in a low, plaintive whinny of fear.

Edward S. Gregory, a local resident, describing the bombardment of Vicksburg, Mississippi, late June 1863:

For forty days and nights without interval the women and children of Vicksburg took calmly and bravely the iron storm. It became at last such an ordinary occurrence that I have seen ladies walk quietly along the streets while the shells burst above them, their heads protected only by a parasol held between them and the sun.

.   .   .

Col. Robert Gould Shaw, the white leader of the 54th Massachusetts "Colored" Regiment, letter to his wife Annie, June 1, 1863, off Cape Hatteras, North Carolina:

The more I think of the passage of the Fifty-fourth through Boston, the more wonderful it seems to me. Just remember our own doubts and fears, and other people's sneering and pitying remarks, when we began last winter, and then look at the perfect triumph of last Thursday. We have gone quietly along, forming the regiment, and at last left Boston amidst a greater enthusiasm than has been seen since the first three-months troops left for the war. Every one I saw, from the Governor's staff (who have always given us rather the cold shoulder) down, had nothing but words of praise for us. Truly, I ought to be thankful for all my happiness, and my success in life so far; and if the raising of coloured troops prove such a benefit to the country, and to the blacks, as many people think it will, I shall thank God a thousand times that I was led to take my share in it.

... **May 18.** Grant commences six-week-long siege of Vicksburg ... **May 22.** Bureau of Colored Troops established in U.S. War Department to recruit blacks into Union army.

(Shaw had initially rejected Gov. John A. Andrew's commission to lead the 54th, but later reconsidered, explaining: "Mother will think I am shirking my duty.")

.   .   .

Mrs. G. Griffin Wilcox, remembering "War Times in Natchez," July 1863:

Federal soldiers had stripped the house of many of its costly furnishings. The edict had gone forth that the "Susette mansion must be blown up with gun-powder and other combustibles, to clear the way for the fort." Excavations were immediately made under and around the grand old edifice. These, together with the cellar, were filled with such immense quantities of powder that when the match was applied to the fuse the explosion was so terrific that half of the window panes in the town were shattered and broken. Such is war.

(Union troops occupied "grand, exclusive, heroic" Natchez, Mississippi, in the summer of 1863. Gen. James Madison Tuttle ordered fortifications built on one of the city's "most magnificent residences.")

... **June 9.** Battle of Brandy Station, Virginia; near-Confederate defeat and humiliation to J.E.B. Stuart in biggest cavalry engagement of war ... **June 14.** Confederate victory at Battle of Winchester, Virginia ... **June 27.** Lincoln names Gen. George G. Meade to replace Hooker as commander of the Army of the Potomac ....

Gettysburg

Augustus Buell, known as the "Boy Cannoneer," recalling the first day's artillery duel at the Battle of Gettysburg, Pennsylvania, July 1, 1863:

Up and down the line men reeling and falling; splinters flying from wheels and axles where bullets hit; in rear, horses tearing and plunging, mad with wounds of terror; drivers yelling, shells bursting, shot shrieking overhead, howling about our ears or throwing up great clouds of dust where they struck; the musketry crashing on the three sides of us; bullets hissing, humming and whistling everywhere; cannon roaring; all crash on crash and peal on peal, smoke, dust, splinters, blood, wreck and carnage indescribable. . . . Every man's shirt soaked with sweat and many of them sopped with blood from wounds not severe enough to make such bulldogs "let go"—bareheaded, sleeves rolled up, faces blackened—oh! if such a picture could be spread on canvas to the life!

Col. Joshua Lawrence Chamberlain, 20th Maine Volunteer Infantry, describing his defense of Little Round Top, second day of the Battle of Gettysburg, July 2, 1863:

The two lines met and broke and mingled in the shock. The crush of musketry gave way to cuts and

. . . **July 1–3.** Battle of Gettysburg, Pennsylvania, largest battle of war and a victory for Union forces; Lee retreats back across Potomac as second and final Northern invasion ends in failure . . . .

thrusts, grapplings and wrestlings. The edge of the conflict swayed to and fro, with wild whirlpools and eddies.
At times I saw around me more of the enemy than of
my own men; gaps opening, swallowing, closing again
with sharp convulsive energy; squads of stalwart men
who had cut their way through us, disappearing as if
translated. All around, strange mingled roar—shouts of
defiance, rally, and desperation; and underneath, mur-
mured entreaty and stifled moans; gasping prayers,
snatches of Sabbath song, whispers of loved names; everywhere men torn and broken, staggering, creeping,
quivering on the earth, and dead faces with strangely
fixed eyes staring stark into the sky. Things which cannot
be told—nor dreamed. How men held on, each one
knows,—not I.

(Chamberlain's bravery on Little Round Top is generally
credited with holding the Union line, turning disaster into
victory, and perhaps even turning the entire tide of the
battle—and the war itself.)

The New York *World*, reporting the Confederate artillery
barrage that preceded Pickett's Charge on the third day's
fighting at Gettysburg, July 3, 1863:

The storm broke upon us so suddenly that soldiers
and officers—who leaped, as it began, from their tents,
or from lazy siestas on the grass—were stricken in their
rising with mortal wounds and died, some with cigars
between their teeth, some with pieces of food in their
fingers, and one at least—a pale young German, from

Pennsylvania—with a miniature of his sister in . . . [his] hands. . . . The earth, torn up in clouds, blinded the eyes of hurrying men; and through the branches of the trees and among the grave-stones of the cemetery a shower of destruction crashed ceaselessly.

(From Seminary Ridge, Lee aimed 115 large guns at Union positions—unleashing "a tempest of orchestral death," in the words of another eyewitness—in what was perhaps the most awesome display of heavy firepower in the entire war.)

Pvt. Warren Lee Goss, U.S.A., describing the Confederate shelling of Union positions before Pickett's Charge at Gettysburg, July 3, 1863:

For an hour and a half crash followed crash. Some of the shot shrieked and hissed, some whistled; some came with muffled growl; some with howls like rushing, circling winds. Some spat and sputtered; others uttered unearthly groans or hoarsely howled their mission of death. Holes like graves were gouged in the earth by exploding shells. The flowers in bloom upon the graves at the Cemetery were shot away. Tombs and monuments were knocked to pieces, and ordinary gravestones shattered in rows. If a constellation of meteoric worlds had exploded above our heads, it would have scarcely been more terrible than this iron rain of death furiously hurled upon us. Over all these sounds were heard the shrieks and groans of the wounded and dying. The uproar of the day previous seemed like silence when compared to this inferno.

Capt. Samuel Fiske, Hancock's Corps:

It was touching to see the little birds, all out of their wits with fright, flying wildly about amidst the tornado of terrible missiles and uttering strange notes of distress. It was touching to see the innocent cows and calves, feeding in the fields, torn in pieces by the shells.

Pvt. Warren Goss, observing Pickett's Charge from behind Union lines, Gettysburg, Pennsylvania, July 3, 1863:

[Pickett's charging men] came on in magnificent order, with the step of men who believed themselves invincible. . . . Solid shot ploughs huge lanes in their close columns. As the enemy approach still nearer, shells burst upon their compact masses. Their shattered lines do not waver, but steadily closing up the gaps of death, come on in magnificent order. With banners waving, with steady step, they sweep on like an irresistible wave of fate [and] they leave behind them a trail of dead and dying, like a swath from the scythe of a mower.

Confederate High-Water Mark

Charles Carleton Coffin, Boston *Journal*, describing the climactic fighting at Gettysburg, July 3, 1863:

Men fire into each other's faces, not five feet apart. There are bayonet-thrusts, sabre-strokes, pistol-shots; cool, deliberate movements on the part of some,—hot, passionate, desperate efforts with others; hand-to-hand contests; recklessness of life; tenacity of purpose; fiery determination; oaths, yells, curses, hurrahs, shoutings; men going down on their hands and knees, spinning round like tops, throwing out their arms, gulping up blood, falling; legless, armless, headless. There are ghastly heaps of dead men. Seconds are centuries; minutes, ages; but the thin line does not break! . . . The Rebel column has lost its power . . . the lines have disappeared like a straw in a candle's flame. The ground is thick with dead, and the wounded are like the withered leaves of autumn. Thousands of Rebels throw down their arms and give themselves up as prisoners. "How inspiring the moment! How thrilling the hour! It is the high-water mark of the Rebellion—a turning point of history and of human destiny!"

(With the Union repulse of Pickett's Charge, the high-water mark of the Confederacy began to ebb. The human cost of the three-day battle was staggering: more than 43,000 casualties on both sides.)

Gen. George Pickett to his fiancee, describing the ill-fated charge he led at Gettysburg, July 3, 1863:

My brave boys were so full of hope and confident of victory as I led them forth! Over on Cemetery Ridge the Federals beheld a scene which has never previously been enacted—an army forming in line of battle in full view, under their very eyes—charging across a space nearly a mile in length, pride and glory soon to be crushed by an overwhelming heartbreak. Well, it is all over now. The awful rain of shot and shell was a sob—a gasp. I can still hear them cheering as I gave the order, "Forward!" the thrill of their joyous voices as they called out, "We'll follow you, Marse George, we'll follow you!" Oh, how faithfully they followed me on—on—to their death, and I led them on—on—on—Oh, God!

Correspondent for the Richmond *Daily Enquirer,* July 3, 1863, Gettysburg, Pennsylvania:

I have never heard such tremendous artillery firing. . . . The very earth shook beneath our feet and the hills and rocks seemed to reel like a drunken man. For one hour and a half this most terrific fire was continued, during which time the shrieking of shells, the crash of falling timber, the fragments of rock flying through the air shattered from the cliffs by solid shot, the heavy muttering from the valley between the opposing armies, the splash of bursting shrapnel, and the fierce neighing of artillery horses, made a picture terribly grand and sublime.

(The artillery bombardment that preceded Pickett's Charge on July 3, 1863—involving more than 200 Union and Confederate guns—was probably the heaviest of the entire war. The charge that came next was perhaps the war's most famous. The correspondent for the Richmond *Daily Enquirer* described its climax:)

On press Pickett's brave Virginians; and now the enemy open upon them, from more than fifty guns, a terrible fire of grape, shell, and canister. On, on they move in unbroken line, delivering a deadly fire as they advance. Now they have reached the Emmetsburgh [*sic*] road, and here they meet a severe fire from the heavy masses of the enemy's infantry, posted behind the stone fence. . . . Now again they advance; they storm the stone fence; the Yankees fly . . . I hear the glad shout of victory. . . . I turn my eyes to the left, and there, all over the plain, in utmost confusion, is scattered this strong division. Their line is broken; they are flying, apparently panic-stricken, to the rear. The gallant Pettigrew is wounded . . . Pickett is left alone . . . Kemper, the grave and chivalrous, reels under a mortal wound. . . . The order is given to fall back.

(Lee's army suffered a staggering 28,000 casualties at Gettysburg; some observers estimated that the caravan of wagons bearing his wounded stretched for 17 miles. "All this," Lee declared, "has been my fault.")

Gen. Abner Doubleday, U.S.A., recalling Lee's unmolested withdrawal from Gettysburg, Pennsylvania, July 4, 1863:

After the Battle Meade had not the slightest desire to recommence the struggle. It is a military maxim that to a flying enemy must be given a wall of steel or a bridge of gold. In the present instance it was unmistakably the bridge of gold that was presented.

. . . **July 4.** Vicksburg surrenders to Grant . . . **July 8.** Union takes Port Hudson, Louisiana . . . .

Gen. Henry W. Halleck to Gen. George G. Meade, July 12, 1863, Washington:

You are strong enough to attack and defeat the enemy before he can effect a crossing. Act upon your own judgement and make your generals execute your orders. Call no council of war. It is proverbial that councils of war never fight. Reinforcements are pushed on as rapidly as possible. Do not let the enemy escape.

(Lee—and his Army of Northern Virginia—"escaped" across the Potomac River the day after this warning was issued to Meade.)

We went into the village this morning and commenc buring our ded and it was a dredful site to behold our ded sogers lay all over the ground as thick as they could lay.

> —Diary entry of a Union cavalryman, July 5, 1863, "Getersburgh"

Gettysburg Baptized with Blood

Oh, you dead, who at Gettysburgh [*sic*] have baptized with your blood the second birth of Freedom in America, how you are to be envied! I rise from a grave whose wet clay I have passionately kissed, and I look up and see Christ spanning this battle-field with his feet and reaching fraternal and lovingly up to heaven. His right hand opens the gates of Paradise—with his left he beckons to these mutilated, bloody, swollen forms to ascend.

—*Samuel Wilkeson, writing in the New York* Times, *July 6, 1863*

(Wilkeson covered the war's greatest battle for the *Times*, knowing that his son was among the Union troops engaging the enemy. After the fighting ended, he went searching for his child, and found him dead. He wrote the beautiful lines above while sitting at his son's grave.)

•   •   •

(The New York Draft riot was the most violent civil disturbance—save for the Civil War itself—in American history. Although its immediate cause was the Lincoln conscription plan, most of its victims were free blacks, who were routinely attacked, burned out, murdered, and mutilated.)

While passing through Clarkson Street ... [I saw] a colored man hanging on a tree, and men and women setting him on fire as he dangled from the branches.

—*A servant girl's breathless report to Morgan Dix, Rector of St. John's Episcopal Church, New York, July 13, 1863*

(Rector Dix confessed twenty years after hearing this grisly story that he refused at first to believe it. Historians still do not know the full extent of casualties among New York's black population during the New York draft riots. But at one point a

... **July 13–16.** Draft Riots break out in New York City. . . . .

mob set fire to the Colored Orphan Asylum on Fifth Avenue, destroyed its furnishings, and even uprooted nearby trees. Only a few hours later, another group of rioters lynched one William Jones, then torched his body—the incident that the servant girl quoted above probably witnessed.)

The negro in his best aspect is repulsive to the white man's instincts; but when he is mixed up as a reason for civil war he becomes odious. Doubtless 'H[orace]. G[reeley, editor of the pro-Emancipation New York *Tribune*].' and his negro allies when hunted through the city last week by disgraceful throngs may have remembered his articles.

—*The New York* Leader, *July 18, 1863*

I saw Susanna Brady, who talked in the most violent manner against the Irish and in favor of the blacks. I feel quite differently, although very sorry and much outraged at the cruelties inflicted. I hope it will give the Negroes a lesson, for since the war commenced, they have been so insolent as to be unbearable. I cannot endure free blacks. They are immoral with all their piety.

—*Maria L. Daly, wife of a New York judge, writing in her diary, July 23, 1863*

Glory at Battery Wagner

At last we have something stirring to record. The 54th, the past week, has proved itself twice in battle. . . . We met the foe on the parapet of Wagner with the bayonet—we were exposed to a murderous fire from the batteries of the fort, from our Monitors and our land batteries, as they did not cease firing soon enough. Mortal men could not stand such a fire, and the assault on Wagner was a failure. . . . The color bearer of the State colors was killed on the parapet. Col. Shaw seized the staff when the standard bearer fell, and in less than a minute after, the Colonel fell himself. When the men saw their gallant leader fall, they made a desperate effort to get him out, but they were either shot down, or reeled in the ditch below. One man succeeded in getting hold of the State color staff, but the color was completely torn to pieces.

—Cpl. James Henry Gooding, 54th Massachusetts Volunteer Infantry, July 20, 1863

(The gallantry of the 54th Massachusetts—"mowed . . . down like grass," according to one eyewitness, as they led the assault on Battery Wagner, near Charleston, South Carolina—came, ironically, on the heels of the racially tinged Draft Riots in New York City earlier in the month, in which blacks were indiscriminately murdered by angry Northerners. The combination of tragic events quickly convinced Northerners that "colored" troops could fight bravely for the Union, and for their own freedom. For generations, however, myth-makers emphasized the heroism of the unit's white colonel, Robert Gould Shaw, and not that of his black troops.)

. . . **July 18.** Union troops repulsed at Battery Wagner, South Carolina, but heroism of 54th Massachusetts "colored" troops proves blacks capable of fighting for own freedom. . . . .

The dead and wounded were piled up in a ditch together sometimes fifty in a heap, and they were strewn all over the plain for a distance of three fourths of a mile. They had two negro regiments and they were slaughtered in every direction. One pile of negroes numbered thirty. Numbers of both white and black were killed on top of our breastworks as well as inside. The negroes fought gallantly, and were headed by as brave a colonel as ever lived. He mounted the breastworks waving his sword, and at the head of his regiment, and he and a negro orderly sergeant fell dead over the inner crest of the works. The negroes were as fine-looking a set as I ever saw.

—Lt. Iredell Jones, surveying the casualties at Battery
Wagner, July 18, 1863

Hannah Johnson to Abraham Lincoln, July 31, 1863, Buffalo, New York:

They tell me some do you will take back the [Emancipation] Proclamation, don't do it. When you are dead and in Heaven, in a thousand years that action of yours will make the Angels sing your praises I know it.

(The writer was the mother of a soldier in the 54th Massachusetts. Lincoln never entertained the idea of backing away from emancipation in order to secure peace.)

Pvt. Samuel R. Watkins, 1st Tennessee Regiment, C.S.A., describing a scene at the attack on Chattanooga, Tennessee, September 8, 1863:

When the cannon ball struck Billy Webster, tearing his arm out of the socket, he did not die immediately, but as we were advancing to the attack, we left him, and the others lying where they fell upon the battlefield; but when we fell back to the place where we had left our knapsacks, Billy's arm had been dressed by Dr. Buist, and he seemed to be quite easy. He asked me Jim Fogey to please write a letter to his parents at home. He wished to dictate the letter. He asked me to please look in his knapsack and get him a clean shirt, and said that he thought he would feel better if he could get rid of the blood that was upon him. I went to hunt for his knapsack and found it, but when I got back to where he was, poor old Billy Webster was dead.

Capt. John William De Forest, 12th Connecticut Volunteers, diary entry, October 10, 1863, Vermilion Bayou, Louisiana:

We forage like the locusts of Revelation. The Western men plunder worse than our fellows. It is pitiful to see how quickly a herd of noble cattle will be slaughtered. Our Negro servants bring in pigs, sheep and fowls, whether we bid it or forbid it. Of course, after the crea-

... **August 21.** Quantrill's Raiders slaughter 150 men, women, and children in Lawrence, Kansas ... **September 2.** Union under Burnside captures Knoxville, Tennessee.

tures are dead and cooked, we eat them to save them, for wasting food is prejudicial to military discipline.

(A prolific novelist and author of travel books and local histories, De Forest won a commission in 1862 and went on, in his words, to see action in "three storming parties, six days of field engagements, and thirty-seven days of siege duty, making forty-six days under fire.")

The soil is soaked and slippery; the mud ankle deep and dotted with "lovely islands in solution;" the streams choked, fords impassible and bridges gone. You attempt to walk, and after reeling like a drunken man attempting to preserve his equilibrium, there are ten chances to one that your locomotive apparatus will fly up, your head down, and a beautiful map of the country done in red clay will be impressed in a most uncomfortable manner in a most inconvenient place. Copyrights of "Life in Tennessee," like these, are dirty cheap all around us.

—*Felix Gregory de Fontaine ("Personnae"), writing in the* Charleston *Daily* Courier, *October 22, 1863*

A "New Birth of Freedom"

The world will little note nor long remember what we say here, but it can never forget what they did here. It is for

us the living, rather, to be dedicated here to the unfin-
ished work which they who fought here have thus far so
nobly advanced. It is rather for us to be here dedicated
to the great task remaining before us—that from these
honored dead we take increased devotion to that cause
for which they gave the last full measure of devotion—
that we here highly resolve that these dead shall not have
died in vain—that this nation, under God, shall have a
new birth of freedom—and that government of the people, by the people, for the people, shall not perish from
the earth.

>   —Abraham Lincoln, Gettysburg, Pennsylvania,
>   November 19, 1863

The cheek of every American must tingle with shame
as he reads the silly flat and dishwatery utterances of the
man who has to be pointed out to intelligent foreigners
as the President of the United States.

>   —The Chicago Times, reacting to Lincoln's Gettysburg
>   Address, November 19, 1863

The dedicatory remarks by President Lincoln will live
among the annals of the war.

>   —The Chicago Tribune, reacting to Lincoln's Gettysburg
>   Address, November 19, 1863

. . . **November 19.** Lincoln delivers Gettysburg Address at consecration of new national
cemetery for battle casualties. . . . .

The President, in a fine, free way, with more grace than is his wont, said his half dozen words of consecration, and the music wailed and he went home through crowded and cheering streets.

—John M. Hay, Lincoln's assistant private secretary,
diary entry, November 20, 1863

• • •

Benjamin Franklin Taylor, Chicago *Evening Journal,* reporting the Battle of Lookout Mountain, November 24, 1863:

Twice I saw it [Sherman's column] swept back in bleeding lines before the furnace-blast, until the russet field seemed some strange page ruled thick with blue and red.

(The all but impregnable, 1100-foot-high Lookout Mountain, southwest of Chattanooga, Tennessee, was finally conquered by federal forces after a full day of bloody fighting.)

Sgt. Frank Phelps, 10th Wisconsin Volunteer Infantry, to his "dear friends," December 2, 1863, from Chattanooga, Tennessee:

While we were on the lines, we were not very far apart, only a little creek between us. The rebs were very friendly, coming down on the bank to trade papers, canteens or anything they could get. I had a New York

Tribune, which I exchanged for an Augusta paper. The next day I exchanged a Wis. State Journal for the Richmond News. They wanted to get playing cards the most. One fellow offered me Greenbacks or gold if I would get him some. He said they had to pay $12 per pack for them and they were good for nothing.

Gen. Daniel Ullman, commander, Corps d'Afrique, to Sen. Henry Wilson, chairman of the Senate Committee on Military Affairs, December 4, 1863:

I fear that many high officials outside of Washington have no other intention than that these men shall be used as diggers and drudges. Now, I am well satisfied from my seven months' intercourse with them that with just treatment they can be made soldiers of as high an average as any in the world. . . . All that is necessary is to give them a fair chance, which has not been done. . . . My own judgement is, that in the great future before us we shall have to draw largely from this element for soldiers, and the sooner we set about it in earnest the better.

(Apparently, reluctance to commit black troops to combat remained entrenched, even six months after the heroism of the 54th Massachusetts at Battery Wagner. Not until June 1864 did the War Department finally order formally that black soldiers be required only "to take their fair share of fatigue duty with white troops.")

. . . **December 8.** Lincoln issues Proclamation of Amnesty and Reconstruction . . . .

1864

IF IT WAS NOT QUITE TOTAL WAR, it was the closest Americans would ever come to it: from Atlanta all the way to the sea, Sherman's devastating march made Georgia howl, leaving cities, towns, and plantations destroyed, and Confederate hopes shattered.

The year had not begun so auspiciously for the Union. Grant's forces met fierce resistance and lost thousands killed and wounded in the Wilderness Campaign in Virginia—ending it no closer to Richmond than when it began.

The only victory that seemed worth celebrating in the North was the largely symbolic duel in which the U.S.S. *Kearsarge* destroyed the audacious Confederate commerce raider *Alabama.* Yet their battle had not even taken place in North America, but off the coast of France. In a

North desperate for good news, the "victory" was none-theless celebrated enthusiastically.

But then Confederates bloodied Sherman at Ken-nesaw Mountain, and in July, Confederate troops came so close to Washington that Lincoln himself came under fire while observing an attack at Fort Stevens just outside the city.

For a time, the only thing that seemed certain in the Union was that Lincoln would not be reelected. He had outmaneuvered attempts by the radical wing of his own party to deny him renomination, but now he faced a far more serious challenge: his opponent in the general election was Gen. George B. McClellan, a military man running on a peace platform. So certain was Lincoln of defeat that he asked his cabinet to sign, sight unseen, a memorandum pledging to cooperate with the next ad-ministration. Then Lincoln worked with black leader Frederick Douglass on a plan to liberate as many slaves as possible before a Democratic president could enter the White House—and, presumably, rescind the Eman-cipation Proclamation.

Military triumphs transformed Lincoln's political for-tunes overnight. General Philip Sheridan made a dra-matic ride to the battlefront and turned the tide at the Battle of Winchester. And Sherman took Atlanta on September 2. On November 8, Lincoln not only won the election, but triumphed over McClellan among the soldiers—whose votes were separately counted—by nearly four to one.

Perhaps the most amazing thing about the 1864 election—about the entire year of 1864—was that the election had taken place at all. Never before had a nation embroiled in civil war staged a democratic vote. "In affording the people the fair opportunity of showing, one to another, and to the world, this firmness and unanimity of purpose," Lincoln declared, "the election has been of vast value to the national cause."

A few weeks later Lincoln received an unexpected "Christmas gift": the city of Savannah, Georgia, conquered by Sherman's unstoppable army. The end was finally in sight.

No, no. Mix them up, mix them up. I am tired of States Rights.

> —Gen. George H. Thomas, U.S.A., in reply to a soldier
> who asked whether the Chattanooga dead should be
> buried according to state, ca. January 1864

I devoured the hindquarters of a muskrat with vindictive relish, and looked with longing upon our adjutant general's young pointer.

> —Report by a South Carolina soldier, early 1864

Our Father who art in Washington, Uncle Abraham be thy name; thy victory won; thy will be done at the South as at the North; gives us this day our daily ration of crackers and pork; and forgive us our shortcomings as

---

. . . **February 1.** Lincoln issues draft call for 500,000 troops . . . **February 27.** First Union captives arrive at Andersonville Prison, Georgia . . . .

we forgive our quartermasters; for thine is the power, the soldiers, and the negroes, for the space of three years, Amen.

—*Anti-Lincoln report in the Chicago* Times, *March 2, 1864*

(The virulently anti-Lincoln *Times* introduced this mock prayer by declaring: "Should he [Lincoln] not be elected, he goes to his political funeral . . . and should he have another term, there will be a national funeral." The newspaper had been briefly shut down by federal troops in June 1863, but reopened to continue its unceasing attacks against the administration.)

Demanding Equal Pay for Black Soldiers

Now it seems strange to me that we do not receive the same pay and rations as the white soldiers. Do we not fill the same ranks? Do we not cover the same space of ground? Do we not take up the same length of ground in a grave-yard that others do? The ball does not miss the black man and strike the white, nor the white and strike the black. But, sir, at that time there is no distinction made; they strike one as much as another. The black men have to go through the same hurling of musketry, and the same belching of cannonading as white soldiers do.

—*Pvt. Edward D. Washington, 54th Mass. Colored Infantry, March 13, 1864*

. . . **March 10.** Lincoln appoints Grant general-in-chief of U.S. armies. . . . .

(Pvt. Washington wrote this angry lament some three weeks after fighting alongside other "colored" troops at the Battle of Olustee, Florida, on February 20, 1864, at which federal casualties numbered some 1,860—or 34% of the Union force.)

William Stillwell, C.S.A., to his wife, Mollie, March 23, 1864, Greenville, Tennessee:

I dreamed a most delightful dream last night. I went to sleep after commending you and our sweet children to God. I was thinking how sweetly you were lying in bed, perhaps not asleep but resting your weary body and thinking of the one on earth most dear, with one [baby] on each side. Oh, how sweet! Thus I was thinking when I fell asleep. I thought we were together and had walked into a garden of flowers. Oh, it was so beautiful! We had been walking hand in hand. We came to a pretty bunch of flowers and stopped to look at them, one on either side. I thought you raised your head up to see what I was doing. I looked at you and you smiled. It pleased me to the heart. I sprang over the flowers to catch you around the waist and just as I caught you, someone called my name and you vanished from my sight and was gone. I awoke. Someone was calling me. Oh, to think that you would treat me so, if you had just stayed until I could have kissed you once more. I would not take anything for my dream.

Susan Bradford, diary entries, April 7 and April 9, 1864, Pine Hill Plantation, Leon County, Florida:

Today I have no shoes to put on. All my life I have never wanted to go barefoot, as most Southern children do. The very touch of my naked foot to the bare ground made me shiver. Lula my Mammy scolds me about this— even yet she claims the privilege of taking me to task when she thinks I need it. . . . I listen to all she has to say but a thought has come to me and I have no time to argue the point. Until the shoes for the army are finished, Mr. McDearnmid will not have time to make any shoes for any one else, this is right, for our dear soldiers must come first in everything.

. . .

Today I have on railroad stockings and slippers. Guess what these slippers are made of? Whenever I go to uncle Richard's I see an old black uncle, hard at work planting shucks and weaving the plaits together into door mats. It seemed to me a lighter braid might be sewed into something resembling shoes, so I picked out the softest shucks and soon had enough to make one slipper. So pleased was I that I soon had a pair of shoes ready to wear. They are a little rough so I have pasted inside a lining of velvet. Everybody laughed, but I feel quite proud.

John L. Ransom, Brigade Quartermaster, 9th Mich. Cavalry, from his diary, Andersonville Prison, March 27–April 9, 1864:

We have issued to us once each day about a pint of beans, or more properly peas, (full of bugs), and three-quarters of a pint of meal, and nearly every day a piece of bacon the size of your two fingers. . . . The pine which we use in cooking is pitch pine, and consequently we are black as negroes. Prison gradually filling from day to day, and situation rather more unhealthy. . . . Take all the exercise we can, drink no water, and try to get along. It is a sad sight to see the men die so fast. New prisoners die the quickest and are buried in the near vicinity, we are told in trenches without coffins. . . . A deadline composed of slats of boards runs round on the inside of the wall, about twelve or fourteen feet from the wall, and we are not allowed to go near it on pain of being shot by the guard. . . . See here, Mr. Confederacy, this is going a little too far. You have no business to kill us off at this rate.

(Nearly 13,000 Union prisoners died of sickness or starvation at Andersonville Prison in southwestern Georgia, at least according to official records; historians have since estimated the casualty toll as far higher. After the war, the Swiss-born commandant of the notorious Confederate prison, Heinrich H. Wirz, was tried for "destroying the lives of prisoners," and executed by hanging.)

Gen. Robert E. Lee to his wife, April 9, 1864, from "Camp":

The bag of socks arrived last evening my dear Mary with your note of the 6th. Who counted them for you? There were only 23 pairs & not 25 as you stated. I opened the bag & counted them myself twice; then sent them over to Major [E. H.] Janney who also counted them & we both made them 23 pairs. I am anxious to get as many socks now as possible, before active operations commence.

Sgt. Achilles V. Clark, 20th Tennessee, C.S.A., describing the fighting at Fort Pillow, Tennessee, April 12, 1864:

The slaughter was awful. The poor deluded negroes would run up to our men fall upon their knees and with uplifted hands scream for mercy but they were ordered to their feet and then shot down. The white men fared but little better. Their fort turned out to be a great slaughter pen. Blood, human blood stood about in pools and brains could have been gathered up in any quantity. I with several others tried to stop the butchery and at one time succeeded but Gen. Forrest ordered them shot down like dogs, and the carnage continued.

Pvt. Daniel Stamps, 13th Tennessee, U.S.A., describing what he saw at Fort Pillow, April 12, 1864:

I saw 2 men shot down while I was under the bluff. They had their hands up; had surrendered, and were begging for mercy . . . saw at least 25 negroes shot down, within 10 or 20 paces from the place where I stood. They had also surrendered, and were begging for mercy.

(When he first heard about the slaughter of Union prisoners at Fort Pillow, Abraham Lincoln ordered an investigation,

. . . **April 12.** Massacre at Fort Pillow, Tennessee, as Confederates under Gen. Nathan Bedford Forrest murder black troops after they surrender . . . .

vowing, "retribution shall . . . surely come." But when he was satisfied that a massacre had indeed taken place, he ordered that "there shall be no similar massacre" against Confederate troops. "Blood cannot restore blood," he concluded, "and government should not act for revenge.")

Charles A. Page, correspondent for the New York *Tribune,* describing the fierce fighting in the Wilderness, May 5, 1864:

The work was at close range. No room in that jungle for maneuvering; no possibility of a bayonet charge, no help from artillery; no help from cavalry; nothing but close, square, severe, face-to-face volleys of fatal musketry. The wounded stream out, and fresh troops pour in. Stretchers pass out with ghastly burdens, and go back reeking with blood for more. Word is brought that the ammunition is failing. Sixty rounds fired in one steady stand-up fight, and that fight not fought out. Boxes of cartridges are placed on the returning stretchers, and the struggle shall not cease for want of ball and powder. Do the volleys grow nearer, or do our fears make them seem so?

(The brutal fight for the thickly forested, boggy area known as The Wilderness, in Virginia, was won, if any side could be declared the victor, by Grant's Union troops, but at a cost of 15% casualties: 17,500 men. Now began Grant's slow march toward Richmond.)

. . . **May 4.** Union troops cross Rapidan River, launch Wilderness Campaign in Virginia
. . . **May 5–6.** Battle of the Wilderness, Virginia . . . .

A. R. Small, 16th Maine Volunteers, remembering the
Wilderness:

May, 1864, initiated a campaign of corduroy roads,
bridges, and earth-works, and until September, there
was a smell of new earth about us, suggestive of planting
time at home. We digged, we tramped; we tramped,
chopped wood, and digged. It was shovel and shoot,
shoot, shovel, and dig. We dug before reveille, and
fought before noon; marched a short distance, and if it
weren't good shooting, piled up the ground. Often the
rebels objected; then we would have a fight, and appropriate their works—if we were the smartest. . . . "Porta-
ble breast-works on the tramp" they called us. We
alternately shouldered spades and muskets, and saw vi-
sions of Richmond and peace in the future.

Pvt. Carlton McCarthy, Richmond Howitzers, Cutshaw's
Battalion Artillery, May 5, 1864, at the Battle of the
Wilderness, Virginia:

The line of battle had been pressed forward and was
in close proximity to the enemy. The thick and tangled
undergrowth prevented a sight of the enemy, but every
man felt he was near. Everything was hushed and still.
No one dared to speak above a whisper. It was evening,
and growing dark. As the men lay on the ground, keenly
sensible to every sound, and anxiously waiting, they
heard the firm tread of a man walking along the line. As
he walked they heard also the jingle-jangle of a pile of
canteens hung around his neck. He advanced with delib-

erate mien to within a few yards of the line and opened a terrific fight by quietly saying, "Can any you fellows tell a man whar he can git some water?" Instantly the thicket was illumined by the flash of a thousand muskets, the men leaped to their feet, the officers shouted, and the battle was begun. Neither side would yield, and there they fought till many died.

Gen. Ulysses S. Grant to a general officer, May 6, 1864, during the Battle of the Wilderness, Virginia:

Oh, I am heartily tired of hearing about what Lee is going to do. Some of you always seem to think he is suddenly going to turn a double somersault, and land in our rear and on both of our flanks at the same time. Go back to your command, and try to think what we are going to do ourselves, instead of what Lee is going to do.

Pvt. Frank Wilkeson, U.S.A., describing the aftermath of the Battle of the Wilderness, Virginia, May 7, 1864:

The wounded soldiers lay scattered among the trees. They moaned piteously. The unwounded troops, exhausted with battle, helped their stricken comrades to the rear. The wounded were haunted with the dread of fire. They conjured the scenes of the previous year, when some wounded men were burned to death, and their hearts well-nigh ceased to beat when they thought they detected the smell of burning wood in the air. The bare prospect of fire running through the woods where they lay helpless, unnerved the most courageous of men, and made them call aloud for help. I saw many wounded soldiers in the Wilderness who hung on to their rifles, and whose intention was clearly stamped on their pallid faces. I saw one man, both of whose legs were broken, lying on the ground with his cocked rifle by his side and his ramrod in his hand, and his eyes set on the front. I knew he meant to kill himself in case of fire—knew it as surely as though I could read his thoughts. The dead men lay where they fell. Their haversacks and cartridges had been taken from their bodies. The battle-field ghouls had rifled their pockets. I saw no dead man that night whose pockets had not been turned inside out.

Gen. Ulysses S. Grant, May 10, 1864, near Spotsylvania Court House, Virginia:

I do not know of any way to put down this Rebellion and restore the authority of the Government except by fighting, and fighting means that men must be killed. If the people of this country expect that the war can be conducted to a successful issue in any other way than by fighting, they must get somebody other than myself to command the army.

("We have lost a good many men," Grant admitted the day he made this statement to a Boston correspondent, "and I suppose I shall be blamed for it.")

... **May 7.** Gen. William T. Sherman launches offensive against Atlanta, Georgia ... **May 8.** Battles begin around Spotsylvania Court House, Virginia. . . . .

Dr. Daniel M. Holt, assistant surgeon, 121st New York
Volunteers, diary entry, May 10, 1864, Spotsylvania, Virginia:

This, to *me*, was the *hardest* day of the fight. One man
was shot a second time while in my arms dressing his
wound, and expired. For an hour bullets, shells and solid
shot flew through our midst as thick as hail. I wonder
why we were not killed.

Gen. Ulysses S. Grant to Secretary of War Edwin M. Stanton,
May 11, 1864, in the field near Spotsylvania Court House,
Virginia:

We have now entered the sixth day of very hard fighting. The result to this time is much in our favor. Our losses
have been heavy as well as those of the enemy. I think the
loss of the enemy must be greater. We have taken over five
thousand prisoners, in battle, while he has taken from us
but few except stragglers. I propose to fight it out on this
line if it takes all summer.

(The next day's fighting at the "Bloody Angle of Spotsylvania"
would test even Grant's bulldog determination; it took a furious, costly charge by no fewer than 24 Union regiments to
dislodge Confederate entrenchments only a few hundred
yards wide.)

William Swinton, the New York *Times*, viewing the Bloody
Angle of Spotsylvania, May 12, 1864:

Nothing during the war has equalled the savage desperation of the struggle . . . and the scene of the conflict
. . . presents a spectacle of horror that curdles the blood

of the boldest. The angle of the works at which [Gen. Winfield Scott] Hancock entered, and for possession of which the savage fight of the day was made, is a perfect Golgotha. In this angle of death the dead and wounded rebels lie, this morning, literally in piles—men in the agonies of death groaning beneath the dead bodies of their comrades. On an area of a few acres in rear of their position lie not less than a thousand rebel corpses, many literally torn to shreds by hundreds of balls, and several with bayonet thrusts through and through their bodies, pierced on the very margins of the parapet, which they were determined to retake or perish in the attempt. The one expression of every man who looks on the spectacle is, "God forbid that I should ever gaze upon such a sight again."

(The human cost of the ferocious day and night of fighting over this one, bloody spot of Virginia earth was ghastly: nearly 12,000 killed and wounded.)

Cpl. John H. B. Payne, 55th Massachusetts Infantry, May 24, 1864 from Morris Island in Charleston harbor, South Carolina:

I am not willing to fight for this Government for money alone. Give me my rights, the rights that this government owes me, the same rights that the white man has. I would be willing to fight three years for this Government without one cent of the mighty dollar.

... **May 12.** Gen. J.E.B. Stuart dies from wounds suffered the previous day at Yellow Tavern, Virginia ... **May 12.** Fierce fighting around the "Bloody Angle," Spotsylvania, Virginia ....

Then I would have something to fight for. Now I am fighting for the rights of white men. . . . Liberty is what I am fighting for; and what pulse does not beat high at the very mention of the name?

Pvt. Frank Wilkeson, 11th New York Battery, recalling the Battle of North Anna, Virginia, May 26, 1864:

The picket-firing and sharpshooting at North Anna was exceedingly severe and murderous. . . . They [sharpshooters] could sneak around trees or lurk behind stumps, or cower in wells or in cellars, and from the safety of their lairs murder a few men. Put the sharpshooters in battle-line and they were no better, no more effective, than the infantry of the line, and they were not half as decent. There was an unwritten code of honor among the infantry that forbade the shooting of men while attending to the imperative calls of nature, and these sharpshooting brutes were constantly violating that rule. I hated sharpshooters, both Confederate and Union . . . and I was always glad to see them killed.

Lt. Col. Horace Porter, attached to Gen. Grant's staff, June 3, 1864:

As I came near one of the regiments which was making preparations for the next morning's assault, I noticed that many of the soldiers had taken off their coats, and seemed to be engaged in sewing up rents in them. This exhibition of tailoring seemed rather peculiar at such a moment, but upon closer examination it was found that the men were calmly writing their names and home addresses on slips of paper, and pinning them to the backs of their coats, so that their dead bodies might be recognized upon the field, and their fate made known to their families at home. They were veterans who knew well from terrible experience the danger which awaited them, but their minds were occupied not with thoughts of shirking their duty, but with preparation for the desperate work of the coming morning. Such courage is more than heroic—it is sublime.

(The Union suffered 7,000 casualties in its dawn attack on Cold Harbor. Grant later conceded, "I regret this assault more than any one I have ever ordered.")

Capt. Oliver Wendell Holmes, Jr., diary entry, June 7, 1864, from the headquarters of the 6th Corps, Virginia:

You show your nose anywhere and sizzle come the bullets at it in less than a twinkling of a bedpost. . . . I started in this thing a boy I am now a man and . . . I can . . . face a great danger coolly enough when I *know* it is a duty.

. . . **June 1–3.** Battle of Cold Harbor, Virginia . . . .

Dr. Daniel M. Holt, assistant surgeon, 121st New York
Volunteers, to his wife, June 10, 1864, in the field before
Cold Harbor, Virginia:

I am on the sick list, *all but reporting* myself so. With
thousands of others I have the Chickahominy [River]
ever to remember with feelings of gratitude,—*grateful because I am not quite dead.* . . . Between the lines (a distance
not greater than thirty rods) the ground was as completely torn up by grape and canister as if it had been
ploughed by the most skillful ploughman. Stealing out
under cover of night, both friend and foe dug little pits
just sufficient to cover their bodies and from these they
picked off such as exposed themselves in any way upon
the works. Here many lay wounded and dead, who could
not be reached for removal, and here the ground was a
complete sepulchre. Scores of putrid bodies defiled the
air—until it became impossible to live so any longer—
consequently the flag of truce was sent in. It was a strange
sight. Five minutes previously it was worth a man's life to
be seen upon the defences, but now hundreds and thousands of both parties swarmed over the neutral ground,
conversing in the most kind and friendly manner.

Sgt. Samuel Clear, 116th Pennsylvania Volunteer Infantry
(Irish Brigade), diary entry, June 7, 1864, Cold Harbor,
Virginia:

The enemy advanced with a white Flag, asking permission to bury their dead, which was granted. We had

an armistice of two hours. The quietness was really oppressive. It positively made us feel lonesome, after a continual racket day and night for so long. We sit on the works and let our legs dangle over on the front and watch the Johnnies carry off their dead comrades in silence, but in a great hurry. Some of them lay dead within twenty feet of our works—the live Rebel looks bad enough in his old torn, ragged Butternut suit, but a dead Rebel looks horrible all swelled up and black in the face. After they were through there was nothing left but stains of Blood, broken and twisted guns, old hats, canteens, every one of them reminders of the death and carnage that reigned a few short hours before.

Col. Theodore Lyman, U.S.A., to his wife, Elizabeth, June 17, 1864, Spotsylvania, Virginia:

People must learn that war is a thing of life and death: if a man won't go to the front he must be shot; but our people can't make up their minds to it; it is repulsive to the forms of thought, even of most of the officers, who willingly expose their own lives, but will shrink from shooting down a skulker [malingerer].

... **June 12.** Grant crosses James River to Petersburg, Virginia ... **June 15.** U.S. House of Representatives defeats constitutional amendment ending slavery ... **June 15.** Pay for black and white privates equalized at $13 per month ....

A Pirate Ship Goes Down Off France

The *Alabama*'s final plunge was a remarkable freak, witnessed by me about 100 yards off. She shot up out of the water bow first and descended on the same line, carrying away with her plunge two of her masts and making a whirlpool of considerable size and strength. The action had lasted one hour and a half. It had taken only that long to end the career of a ship which had made history for the better part of two years, and whose gallant deeds have secured for her a permanent niche in the hall of maritime fame.

> —*Admiral Raphael Semmes, C.S.A., remembering the sinking of his ship, the* Alabama, *off Cherbourg, France, June 19, 1864*

(Although this sea battle did not even take place in America, the widely reported sinking of the commerce raider *Alabama* by the *U.S.S. Kearsarge* was received joyously by Northerners.)

. . .

Henry E. Schaefer, musician with the 103rd Illinois, in a letter to his wife, June 23, 1864:

I can look at a dead man or help a wounded man from the field and think no more of it than I would of eating my dinner. I am ashamed to say it but I have seen so much of it that in one sens [*sic*] of the word I have become hardened and it does not affect me but little to walk over the field of strife and behold its horrors.

. . . **June 19.** U.S.S. *Kearsarge* destroys Confederate ship *Alabama* off the coast of Cherbourg, France. . . . .

Capt. Oliver Wendell Holmes, Jr., 20th Massachusetts Volunteers, to his parents, June 24, 1864, near Petersburg, Virginia:

These last few days have been very bad . . . hot & nasty as Orcus—I think there is a kind of heroism in the endurance. . . . I tell you many a man has gone crazy since this campaign began from the terrible pressure on mind and body. . . . I hope to pull through but don't know yet—Goodbye[.]

(Holmes was present on July 12, 1864 when, for the second consecutive day, a curious and apparently fearless Abraham Lincoln travelled to Fort Stevens, outside Washington, to observe first-hand an attack by Confederate Gen. Jubal Early. Standing high above the parapets, easily identifiable in his trademark stovepipe hat, Abraham Lincoln must have made a tempting target for the enemy raiders, until Holmes warned the President, "Get down, you fool!" Coming under fire for the first and only time during the war, Lincoln may well have been saved by Holmes' bold admonition that day.)

Correspondent of the Cincinnati *Commercial,* observing the battlefield of Ezra Church, near Atlanta, July 28, 1864:

[The dead were] scattered as they had fallen . . . in all attitudes of fierce despair, of agony, or placid repose. . . .

. . . **June 27.** Confederates defeat Sherman at Battle of Kennesaw Mountain, Georgia . . . **July 4.** Lincoln pocket vetoes Wade-Davis Bill, which would have imposed harsh conditions on defeated Confederate states . . . **July 11–12.** Confederates threaten Washington suburbs; Lincoln witnesses attack at Fort Stevens . . . **July 17.** Commencement of battles for Atlanta . . . **July 28.** Battle of Ezra Church, Georgia . . . .

All along a little rivulet of muddy water the poor wretches had crawled down into it, in their dying agony, to quench their thirst, and made its banks bloody from their wounds. One had snatched in his feeble hand a bunch of dry leaves with which he had vainly attempted to staunch the blood with which his life was flowing slowly but certainly away.

(Confederate forces went on the offensive at Ezra Church, Georgia, but suffered as many as 5,000 casualties while failing to slow the momentum of Sherman's dogged pursuit of the nearby hub of Atlanta.)

Clara Barton, diary entry, July 29, 1864:

If I were to attempt to tell you how hard we had wrought during the last four or five weeks in the sun and dust, to make a comfortable homelike resting place for the poor sufferers who fell back into our hands, you would only think me egotistical but, if I tell you that I try to see that every one of the many hundreds has the proper nourishment each day, and to answer every want that reaches me—stand beside the three or four death beds which number themselves with us each day—and stand by each lonely grave as the earth is thrown in, where some weeping mother, wife, or sister would stand if she might, you will say with great justice, that it is my duty to do these things.

(Seventeen years after writing this letter from one of the countless battlefield hospitals at which she labored, Clara Barton founded the American Red Cross.)

Sara Rice Pryor, August 1864, Petersburg, Virginia:

The month of August in the besieged city passed like a dream of terror. The weather was intensely hot and dry, varied by storms of thunder and lightning—when the very heavens seemed in league with the thunderbolts of the enemy. Our region was not shelled continuously. One shot from "our own gun," as we learned to call it, would be fired as if to let us know our places; this challenge would be answered from one of our batteries, and the two would thunder away for five or six hours.

(The interminable, nightmarish siege of Petersburg would last until April 1, 1865, when Grant's superior Union forces finally overpowered the thin Confederate defenses that had successfully resisted for so long. In all, the Petersburg campaign exacted a staggering 70,000 casualties on both sides.)

Correspondent for the Petersburg (Va.) *Daily Express,* August 1, 1864:

The sides and bottom of the chasm were literally lined with Yankee dead, and the bodies lay in every conceivable position. In one spot we noticed a corporal of infantry, a sergeant of artillery, and a big, burly negro, piled one upon top of the other. Some had evidently been killed with the butts of muskets as their crushed

----

. . . **July 30.** Battle of the Crater, Petersburg, Virginia, ends in Union defeat after federals explode huge mine beneath Confederate works. . . . .

skulls and badly mashed faces too plainly indicated, while the greater portion were shot, great pools of blood having flowed from their wounds and stained the ground.

(The Battle for the Crater at Petersburg on July 30, 1864, was for the Union a technological triumph and, according to Ulysses S. Grant, a "stupendous failure" as a military action. Federal forces successfully dug a 500-foot-long trench under Confederate positions, filled it with gunpowder, and detonated it in the most spectacular display of firepower of the entire war: 300 surprised Confederates were killed or wounded. But when Union forces charged into the resulting crater, the enemy regrouped and counterattacked, surrounding and trapping thousands of white and black soldiers inside the hideous pit. Many were brutally killed in hand-to-hand combat.)

Pvt. Andrew McCornack, 127th Illinois Volunteer Infantry, August 1, 1864, "near Atlanta":

They [the Rebels] came very near taking our whole company, but when I saw that we were surrounded, I thought I would try and get away. I started as fast as Jim Shank's horses could travel. The rebs kept hollering, "Halt, you son-of-a-bitch," but I could not see it, and got away all right, and joined the regiment, which was pouring volleys into them the best they knew how. . . . The next morning we found 650 dead in front of the 15th Corps.

Farragut at Mobile Bay

Damn the torpedoes! Full speed ahead!

—*Adm. David G. Farragut at Mobile Bay, August 5, 1864*

(Farragut this day defied withering fire from Confederate forts along the shore, and the peril of deadly torpedoes haunting the waters below, as his fleet stormed into Mobile Bay. Lashed to the rigging of his flagship—so he would remain upright even if wounded—the defiant admiral went on to seize or destroy enemy ships, silence the forts, and conquer the port of Mobile for the Union. Astonishingly, Farragut was 63 years old at the time.)

Gen. Ulysses S. Grant to Rep. Elihu Washburne, August 16, 1864, City Point, Virginia:

The rebels have now in their ranks their last man. The little boys and old men are guarding prisoners, guarding rail-road bridges and forming a good part of their garrisons for intrenched positions. A man lost by them cannot be replaced. They have robbed the cradle and the grave equally to get their present force. Besides what they lose in frequent skirmishes and battles they are now loosing from desertions and other causes at least one regiment per day. With this drain upon them the end is visible if we will but be true to ourselves. Their only hope now is a divided North. This might give them reinforcements from Tenn. Ky. Maryland and Mo. whilst it would weaken us. With the draft quietly enforced the enemy would become dispondent and would make but little resistance. I have no doubt but the enemy are exceedingly anxious to hold out until after the Presidential election. They have many hopes from its effects. They hope a counter revolution. They hope the election of the peace candidate. In fact, like McCawber [the Dickens character in *David Copperfield*], the[y] hope *something* to turn up.

(Portions of this letter were publicly circulated to help Lincoln's reelection effort. Grant approved their use, although privately he joked that "to attempt to answer all the charges . . . against him will be like setting a maiden to work to prove her chastity.")

The wretched prisoners burrowed in the ground like moles to protect themselves from the sun. It was not safe to give them material to build shanties as they might use it for clubs to overcome the guard. These underground huts . . . were alive with vermin and stank like charnel houses. Many of the prisoners were stark naked, having not so much as a shirt to their backs. . . . Father Hamilton said that . . . he saw some of them die on the ground without a rag to lie on or a garment to cover them. . . . It is dreadful. My heart aches for the poor wretches, Yankees though they are, and I am afraid God will suffer some terrible retribution to fall upon us for letting such things happen.

—*Eliza Frances Andrews, journal entry, summer 1864, near Andersonville, Georgia*

Annie Davis to Abraham Lincoln, August 25, 1864,
Belair, Maryland:

Mr president It is my Desire to be free. to go to see my people on the eastern shore. my mistress wont let me you will please let me know if we are free. and what i can do. I write to you for advice.

(No response to this letter is known. Lincoln's Emancipation Proclamation had not affected slaves in Union states such as Maryland. But by this time, Lincoln had endorsed a constitutional amendment abolishing slavery everywhere.)

George Templeton Strong, diary entry, August 29, 1864,
New York City:

To office of Provost Marshal of my district this morning (Captain Manierre), where, after waiting an hour, I purveyed myself a substitute, a big "Dutch" boy of twenty or thereabouts, for the moderate consideration of $1,100. Thus do we approach the alms-house at an accelerating rate of speed. My *alter ego* could make a good soldier if he tried. Gave him my address, and told him to write to me if he found himself in the hospital, or in trouble, and that I would try to do what I properly could to help him. I got myself exempted at this high price because I felt all day as if some attack of illness were at hand.

(Substitution was outlawed in the manpower-starved Confederacy in 1863, but continued to flourish, to widespread criticism, in the North. A rich conscript could hire a soldier to fight in his place. The writer was a prominent attorney, with no plausible excuse for exemption from service except nearsightedness—and wealth.)

Mary Boykin Chesnut, diary entry, September 1, 1864, Columbia, South Carolina:

The battle is raging at Atlanta—our fate hanging in the balance. Atlanta gone. Well—that agony is over. Like David when the child was dead, I will get up from my knees, will wash my face and comb my hair. No hope. We will try to have no fear.

Miss Mollie E. to Abraham Lincoln, September 9, 1864, Gallia Furnace, Ohio:

There is fifteen young Ladies of the most worthy families that is in this part of the country we wish to do something for our Country we have been wanting to do something Ever since this Cruel war broke out but Circumstances will not permit it. but we cannot wait any longer we must do something[.] We have sent all that is Near and dear to us and we must help them in some way[.] We are willing to be sworn in for one year or more eny lenght of time it makes no difference to us. But we must do something to help, save that Beautifull Flag that

... **September 2.** Sherman takes Atlanta.......................................

has Waved so long, oer the Land of he Free and the home of the brave[.]

Mayor James M. Calhoun of Atlanta to Gen. William T. Sherman, September 11, 1864, protesting the Union general's order to evacuate the city:

How is it possible for the people still here (mostly women and children) to find any shelter? And how can they live through the winter in the woods—no shelter or subsistence, in the midst of strangers who know them not, and without the power to assist them much, if they were willing to do so? This is but a feeble picture of the consequences of this measure. You know the woe, the horrors, and the suffering, cannot be described by words; imagination can only conceive of it, and we ask you to take these things into consideration . . . and what has this *helpless* people done, that they should be driven from their homes, to wander strangers and outcasts, and exiles, and to subsist on charity?

Gen. William T. Sherman to Mayor James M. Calhoun of Atlanta, September 12, 1864, from the field, near the city:

You cannot qualify war in harsher terms than I will. War is cruelty, and you cannot refine it; and those who brought war into our country deserve all the curses and maledictions a people can pour out. . . . You might as well appeal against the thunder-storm as against these terrible hardships of war. They are inevitable, and the only way the people of Atlanta can hope once more to live in peace and quiet at home, is to stop the war, which can only be done by admitting that it began in error and is perpetuated in pride. We don't want your negroes, or your horses, or your houses, or your lands, or any thing you have, but we do want and will have a just obedience to the laws of the United States. That we will have, and if it involves the destruction of your improvements, we cannot help it. . . . I want peace, and believe it can only be reached through union and war, and I will ever conduct war with a view to perfect and early success. But, my dear sirs, when peace does come, you may call on me for any thing. Then will I share with you the last cracker, and watch with you to shield your homes and families against danger from every quarter. Now you must go, and take with you the old and feeble, feed and nurse them, and build for them in more quiet places, proper habitations to shield them against the weather until the mad passions of men cool down, and allow the Union and peace once more to settle over your old homes in Atlanta.

F. Kendall to Jefferson Davis, September 16, 1864, Greenville, Georgia:

Mr. President. Is it not time now to enlist the negroes? I have been in favor of it ever since the enemy commenced it, & have feared no effort would be made on our side until it was too late. It is now our only resource to augment the army. My plan is to conscribe them & force them into the army, all between Sixteen & fifty-five, upon the condition if necessary, of freedom after the war. . . . I am almost inclined to believe that they would do it if *emancipation* was the *condition*.

(The Confederacy continued to refuse to entertain the idea of recruiting blacks for their armies, even as black enlistments swelled Union ranks.)

A Plea for Black Officers

We want black commissioned officers; and only because we want men we can understand and who can understand us. We want men whose hearts are truly loyal to the rights of man. . . . We want to demonstrate our ability to rule, as we have demonstrated our willingness to obey. In short, we want simple justice.

> —*A letter to the editor from an anonymous "Sergeant" in the 54th Mass. Infantry, stationed at Morris Island, South Carolina, and published in* The Liberator *on October 4, 1864*

Gen. William T. Sherman to George B. McClellan, October 11, 1864:

I think I understand the purpose of the South properly and that the best way to deal with them is to meet them fair & square on any issue—we must fight them.

Cut into them—not talk [to] them, and pursue till they cry enough. If we relax one bit we could never hold up our head again. They would ride us roughshod.

(McClellan—then the Democratic candidate for President—had written to congratulate Sherman for capturing Atlanta, a victory McClellan likely knew had crippled his chance to defeat Lincoln.)

Col. Charles Russell Lowell, Jr., 2nd Massachusetts Cavalry, October 17, 1864, near Belle Grove, Virginia:

I don't want to be shot until I've had a chance to come home. I have no idea that I shall be hit, but I *want* so much not to now, that it sometimes frightens me.

(Within days, Lowell's forces would be engaged in the Battle of Cedar Creek. Lowell himself was struck down by a Confederate sharpshooter and died the next day.)

Artist James Taylor, witnessing Sheridan's Ride, October 19, 1864:

Now the big, black, white-fetlocked Rienzi, bearing the general, thunders by like a whirlwind. He is

. . . **September 19.** Gen. Philip Sheridan defeats Gen. Jubal Early for Union victory at Winchester, Virginia . . . **October 19.** Shenandoah Valley campaign ends with Confederate loss at Cedar Creek, after Sheridan inspires troops with famous ride to the front from Winchester . . . .

braced well back in his saddle, his body forward bent and his feet in the hooded stirrups are on a line with the animal's breast, that being the only position in which his short legs could insure his seat on the rough Racker.

Sheridan's Ride

What was done? What to do? A glance told him both,
Then, striking his spurs with a terrible oath,
He dashed down the line 'mid a storm of huzzas,
And the wave of retreat checked its course there, because
The sight of the master compelled it to pause,
With foam and with dust the black charger was gray;
By the flash of his eye, and the red nostril's play,
He seemed to the whole great army to say,
"I have brought you Sheridan all the way
  From Winchester down to save the day!"

—*Thomas Buchanan Read,* Sheridan's Ride, *October 1864*

(Gen. Philip H. Sheridan's breathless, inspiring ride to the front from Winchester, Virginia, helped turn a probable Union defeat at the Battle of Cedar Creek into an inspiring Union victory on October 19, 1864—although Read's immensely popular poem probably exaggerated its impact.)

Counting the Votes

John M. Hay, assistant secretary to President Lincoln, diary entry, election day, November 8, 1864:

The President sent over the first fruits to Mrs. Lincoln. He said, "She is more anxious than I. . . ." Despatches kept coming in all the evening, showing a splendid triumph in Indiana, showing steady, small gains all over Pennsylvania. . . . Towards midnight we had supper, provided by [Thomas] Eckert [Superintendent of the War Department telegraph]. The President went awkwardly and hospitably to work shovelling out the fried oysters. He was most agreeable and genial all the evening in fact. . . . Capt Thomas came up with a band about half-past two, and made some music and a small hifalute. The President answered from the window with rather unusual dignity and effect & we came home. W[ard]. H[ill]. L[amon]. [Marshal of the District of Columbia] came to my room to talk. . . . He took a glass of whiskey and then, refusing my offer of a bed, went out &, rolling himself up in his cloak, lay down at the President's door; passing the night in that attitude of touching and dumb fidelity, with a small arsenal of pistols & bowie knives around him. In the morning he went away leaving my blankets at my door, before I or the President were awake.

. . . **November 1.** Maryland abolishes slavery . . . **November 8.** Lincoln reelected President of the United States . . . .

James M. Scovel to Abraham Lincoln, November 9, 1864, Philadelphia:

George Washington made the Republic. Abraham Lincoln will save it[.]

(Lincoln defeated George B. McClellan for the presidency, winning 55 percent of the popular vote and 212 of 233 electoral votes. Perhaps most gratifying of all, Lincoln won 78% of the separately counted soldiers' vote, to only 22% for the former general.)

Abraham Lincoln, response to a victory serenade, November 10, 1864, the White House, Washington:

We can not have free government without free elections; and if the rebellion could force us to forego, or postpone a national election, it might fairly claim to have already conquered and ruined us. . . . It has demonstrated that a people's government can sustain a national election, in the midst of a great civil war . . . [that] he who is most opposed to treason, can receive most of the people's vote. . . . May I ask those who have not differed with me, to join with me, in the same spirit towards those who have?

George B. McClellan to his mother, Elizabeth, November 11, 1864:

The smoke has cleared away and we are beaten. . . . Personally I am glad that the dreadful responsibility of the government of the nation is not to devolve upon my shoulders.

Ernest Duvergier de Hauranne, French visitor to America,
journal entry, November 13, 1864, Columbus, Ohio:

Don't think that I'm excusing the Rebels, but a civil
war, when it has lasted as long as this one has, is the
fiercest and most merciless of all wars. If people easily
forgive foreigners, they vow eternal hatred for the enemy
in their own family, in their own home. Think of the be-
havior of both sides in this war, of the murders and pillag-
ing on both sides, of the terrible practice of shooting
prisoners, of the even more terrible custom of killing
dozens of innocent prisoners in reprisal of each new out-
rage by the enemy. Even when, in judging these atrocities,
you make allowance for the Americans' normal brutality,
you can appreciate how deeply the two sides have come to
detest each other. I doubt that more corpses can ever fill
in the river of blood that separates them.

Sherman's March Begins

Gen. William T. Sherman, November 16, 1864:

Behind us lay Atlanta, smouldering and in ruins, the
black smoke rising high in air, and hanging like a pall
over the ruined city. Away off in the distance . . . was the
rear of [Gen. O. O.] Howard's column, the gun-barrels
glistening in the sun, the white-topped wagons stretch-

... **November 16.** Sherman begins his march from Atlanta to the sea. . . . .

ing away to the south; and right before us the Four-teenth Corps, marching steadily and rapidly, with a cheery look and swinging pace, that made light of the thousands of miles that lay between us and Richmond. Some band, by accident, struck up the anthem of "John Brown's soul goes marching on;" the men caught up the strain, and never before or since have I heard the chorus of "Glory, glory, hallelujah!" done with more spirit, or in better harmony of time and place.

Maj. James Connolly, 123rd Illinois, on Sherman's march from Atlanta to the sea, ca. November 1864:

Our men are foraging on the country with the great-est liberality. Foraging parties start out in the morning; they go where they please, seize wagons, mules, horses, and harness; make the negroes of the plantation hitch up, load the wagons with sweet potatoes, flour, meal, hogs, sheep, chickens, turkeys, barrels of molasses and in fact everything good to eat, and sometimes consider-able that's good to drink. Our men are living well as they could at home.

(Several weeks after taking Atlanta on September 2, 1864, William T. Sherman marched 62,000 men some 250 miles to the outskirts of Savannah, near the Atlantic coast, in just 26 days, ordering that his army "forage liberally on the country during the march." Sherman's troops laid waste to a swath of Georgia land 60 miles wide—at a reported cost of $100 mil-lion in damage.)

Gen. William T. Sherman, Special Field Orders of November 9, 1864, in the field, Kingston, Georgia:

Should guerrillas or bushwackers molest our march, or should the inhabitants burn bridges, obstruct roads, or otherwise manifest local hostility, then army commanders should order and enforce a devastation more or less relentless, according to the measure of such hostility.

(With these orders, Sherman's brutal, triumphant, and controversial march to the sea commenced. The general was convinced that his daring movement east would not only "make Georgia howl," but "demonstrate the vulnerability of the South.")

Maj. George W. Nichols, U.S.A., with Sherman's army on its march to the sea, November 29, 1864, near Johnston, Georgia:

The most pathetic scenes occur upon our line of march daily and hourly. Thousands of Negro women join the column, some carrying household goods, and many of them carrying children in their arms, while older boys and girls plod by their side. All these women and children are ordered back, heartrending though it may be to refuse them liberty. One begs that she may go to see her husband and children at Savannah. Long

---

. . . **November 22.** Sherman's troops capture Milledgeville, Georgia . . . **November 29.** Indian massacre at Sand Creek, Colorado. . . . .

years ago she was forced from them and sold. Another has heard that her boy was in Macon, and she is "done gone with grief goin' on four years." But the majority accept the advent of the Yankees as the fulfillment of the millennial prophecies. The "day of jubilee," the hope and prayer of a lifetime, has come. They can not be made to understand that they must remain behind, and they are satisfied only when General Sherman tells them, as he does every day, that we shall come back for them some time, and that they must be patient until the proper hour of deliverance occurs.

A Union recruit on Sherman's march, ca. November 1864:

Around me is the gibber of reckless men & I am compelled to Listen day and night to their profanity, filthy talk and vulgar songs. I have some conception how Lot felt in Sodom when he had to listen to and be cursed by the filthy conversation of the wicked.

Pvt. Samuel Watkins, 1st Tennessee Regiment, C.S.A., recalling the Battle of Franklin, Tennessee, November 30, 1864:

It beggars description. I will not attempt to describe it. I could not. The death-angel was there to gather its last harvest. It was the grand coronation of death. Would that I could turn the page. But I feel, though I did so,

. . . **November 30.** Battle of Franklin, Tennessee, ends in disaster for Confederate Gen. John Bell Hood. . . . .

that page would still be there, teeming with its scenes of horror and blood. . . . O, my God! What did we see! It was a grand holocaust of death. Death had held high carnival there that night. The dead were piled the one on the other all over the ground. . . . Horses, like men, had died game on the gory breast-works. . . . I cannot tell the number of others killed and wounded. God alone knows that. We'll all find out on the morning of the final resurrection.

(The Confederate frontal assault on the Union lines at Nashville ended in disaster; more than 6,200 fell—making it a costlier repulse than Pickett's Charge at Gettysburg.)

Mary Boykin Chesnut, diary entry, December 19, 1864, Columbia, South Carolina:

The deep waters closing over us. And we are—in this house—like the outsiders at the time of the Flood. We care for none of these things. We eat, drink, laugh, dance, in lightness of heart!!!

A New Hampshire officer observing the bungled execution of deserters near Laurel Hill, Virginia, December 21, 1864:

We looked toward the graves [after a firing squad had shot at five convicted, blindfolded deserters], but to our astonishment each man yet remained standing, showing

---

. . . **December 6.** Lincoln names Salmon P. Chase chief justice of the supreme court.

conclusively that the detail had fired high. The second or reserve detail was at once marched into position . . . and at the same signal the smoke puffed from their carbines, and their fire proved more accurate, but not entirely effective. The prisoners all fell. Three were dead, while two were trying hard to rise again, and one of them even got upon his knees, when a bullet from the revolver of the provost marshall sent him down. Again he attempted to rise, getting upon his elbow and raising his body nearly to a sitting posture, when a second bullet in the head from the marshall's revolver suddenly extinguished what little life was left and a third shot put out the life of the second prisoner, thus ending the execution.

(During the Civil War 278,000 Union and 105,000 Confederate men deserted. If they returned or were captured, deserters were subject to court-martial, prison, or death—although relatively few were executed.)

Gen. William T. Sherman to Abraham Lincoln, December 22, 1864:

I beg to present to you as a Christmas gift the City of Savannah with 150 heavy guns & plenty of ammunition & also about 25.000 bales of cotton.

(Lincoln replied: "When you were about leaving Atlanta for the Atlantic coast, I was *anxious*, if not fearful. . . . Now, the

December 15–16. Union under Gen. George H. Thomas defeats Confederates at Nashville, effectively ending the war in the west. . . . .

undertaking being a success, the honor is all yours. . . . Please make my grateful acknowledgements to your whole army, officers and men.")

. . . **December 21.** Sherman captures Savannah, Georgia. . . . .

1865

ON A SUNNY SPRING AFTERNOON in early April, the most recognizable man in the Confederate military service rode slowly, totally unguarded, past armed Union troops—and no one fired a shot. For on this day, Robert E. Lee was riding toward Appomattox Court House, Virginia, to surrender his army to Ulysses S. Grant. The war was finally over.

Lee had exhausted all his resources—strategy, guile, grit, and inspiration—to forestall the inevitable. But by early April he was forced to urge the Davis government to abandon Richmond, and a few days later Lincoln himself walked the conquered capital's smoldering streets—greeted there as a deliverer by the city's now-emancipated slaves while fearful whites hid solemnly behind their curtains.

Charleston and Columbia in South Carolina were already in ruins, and towns in North Carolina were falling like dominoes. Meanwhile, the Union Congress had acted to forward to the states a constitutional amendment abolishing slavery everywhere. There was no turning back.

Grant proceeded to tighten the noose around Petersburg, and when that city, too, fell on April 3, a trapped Lee prepared to make his final stand around Appomattox. It was Grant who proposed instead that his foe abandon the fight—to prevent, he said, "any further effusion of blood." Two days later, Lee, gleaming in his fancy dress uniform, sword at his side, sat down with Grant, who was garbed only in the plain blouse of a private with the insignia of a lieutenant general.

Grant's terms were generous—echoing the "malice toward none" sentiments Lincoln had expressed in his second inaugural address the previous month. Within a few days, Lee's army stacked its arms and headed home. Jubilation erupted throughout the North.

And then, barely a week after the joy, came the sorrow—a "noon" and a "midnight" of emotion, as one man put it, "without a space between!" On the night of April 14, while enjoying a comedy at Ford's Theatre in downtown Washington, Lincoln was shot from behind by the celebrated actor John Wilkes Booth. The next morning, the last casualty of the Civil War died without regaining consciousness. "In one hour, under the blow of a single bereavement," declared Rev. Henry Ward Beecher, "joy lay without a pulse, without a gleam, or breath. . . . Did ever so many hearts, in so brief a time, touch two such boundless feelings?"

Jefferson Davis lived on—at first, ignominiously. Captured in Georgia wearing his wife's overcoat as a disguise, the Confederacy's first and only president was for a time mercilessly lampooned by his detractors. But when his captors at Ft. Monroe shackled him, he emerged a living martyr to the Lost Cause—no less important a figure to the South than the mythified Lincoln had become to the North.

Lee went on to urge sectional reconciliation and became a college president. Grant proclaimed "let us have peace" and was elected to the White House. But some veterans proved unreconstructable. On a plantation near Richmond, the old secessionist fire-eater Edmund Ruffin—the man who had fired the first shot on Fort Sumter four years earlier—now reiterated his eternal hatred of Yankees and shot himself to death.

It would take generations to meet the challenge Lincoln had issued on Inauguration Day, March 4: "to bind up the nation's wounds." And even now, some still hear the guns.

Col. Charles B. Fox, 55th Mass. Colored Regiment, describing his entrance into conquered Charleston, South Carolina, February 17, 1865:

Words would fail to describe the scene which those who witnessed it will never forget,—the welcome given to a regiment of colored troops by their people redeemed from slavery. As shouts, prayers, and blessings resounded on every side, all felt that the hardships and dangers of the siege were fully repaid. The few white inhabitants left in the town were either alarmed or indignant, and generally remained in their houses; but the colored people turned out *en masse*. . . . Cheers, blessings, prayers, and songs were heard on every side. Men and women crowded to shake hands with men and officers. . . . On through the streets of the rebel city passed the column, on through the chief seat of the slave power, tottering to its fall. Its walls rung to the chorus of manly voices singing "John Brown," "Babylon is Falling," and the "Battle-Cry of Freedom". . . . It was one of those occasions which happen but once in a lifetime, to be lived over in memory forever.

Charles Carleton Coffin, writing in The Boston *Journal* from Charleston, South Carolina:

The city is a ruin. The tall rank weeds of last year's growth, dry and withered now, rattle in every passing breeze in the very heart of that city which, five years ago, was so proud and lofty in spirit. Lean and hungry dogs skulk amid the tenantless houses. . . . Spiders spin their webs in counting houses.

. . . **January 15.** Union captures Fort Fisher, North Carolina . . . **January 31.** House of Representatives finally approves constitutional amendment abolishing slavery . . . **February 1.** Lincoln's home state—Illinois—becomes first to ratify 13th Amendment to Constitution, abolishing slavery . . . **February 1.** Sherman begins march through Carolinas . . . **February 13.** Confederacy reluctantly approves recruitment of slaves as soldiers, with approval of owners . . . **February 17.** Union army captures and destroys Columbia, South Carolina . . . **February 17.** Union army marches into Charleston, South Carolina . . . .

William Gilmore Simms, recalling the Union conquest of
Columbia, South Carolina, February 17–19, 1865:

Day by day brought to the people of Columbia tidings
of atrocities committed, and more extended progress.
Daily did long trains of fugitives line the roads, with
wives and children, and horses and stock and cattle,
seeking refuge from the pursuers. Long lines of wagons
covered the highways. Half-naked people cowered from
the winter under bush tents in the thickets, under the
eaves of houses, under the railroad sheds, and in old cars
left them along the route. All these repeated the same
story of suffering, violence, poverty, and nakedness.
Habitation after habitation, village after village—one
sending up its signal flames to the other, presaging for it
the same fate—lighted the winter and midnight sky with
crimson horrors.

(Simms, a well-known writer, collected his bitter recollections
of the federal march through his home state—"scenes of
license, plunder, and general conflagration"—into an angry
pamphlet published later that year, *Sack and Destruction of the
City of Columbia, South Carolina*.)

Brig. Gen. Joshua Lawrence Chamberlain to his parents,
February 20, 1865:

I owe the Country three years service: It is a time when
every man should stand by his guns. And I am not scared
or hurt enough yet to be willing to face the rear, when
other men are marching to the front. It is true my incom-

plete recovery from my wounds would make a more quiet life desirable, & when I think of my young & dependent family the whole strength of that motive to make the most of my life comes over me. But there is no promise of life in peace, & no decree of death in war. And I am so confident of the sincerity of my motives that I can trust my own life & the welfare of my family in the hands of Providence.

(Chamberlain, hero of the Little Round Top at Gettysburg, for which he won a Congressional Medal of Honor 30 years later, was wounded four different times in the months that followed, and few expected his return to active service. Grant later honored him by choosing him to accept the formal surrender of Lee's troops at Appomattox. He lived until 1914, serving four terms as Governor of Maine.)

Charlotte St. Julien Ravenel, diary entry, March 1, 1865, Pooshee Plantation, Berkeley County, South Carolina:

Everything went on as usual until nine o'clock at night when we heard several pistol shots in the negro yard. I ran up stairs to tell Pennie who had gone to bed and by the time I got back we heard a noise at the back door; our hearts sank when we heard them talking, for they were negroes without an officer, what we had always dreaded. They asked for the master of the house, and when Grand Pa went out, they asked him in the most insolent manner for his horses, wagons, meat, and poultry. . . . It made our blood curdle to hear our aged

... **February 22.** Tennessee abolishes slavery. . . . .

relative spoken to in the manner they did. We were all in the hall and heard everything that went on below. After some very impudent language we heard a gun click. I will never forget that moment as long as I live. The wretch had his gun pointed at Grand Pa, and though we found out afterwards that they did not dare to take life, we did not know it. . . . We have to do our own cooking now. . . . The field negroes are in a dreadful state; they will not work, but either roam the country, or sit in their houses. At first they all said they were going, but have changed their minds. . . . I do not see how we are to live in this country without any rule or regulation. We are afraid now to walk outside of the gate.

(After the Union occupied Charleston, white and black troops alike were ordered out into the environs in search of food and other supplies. To the federal troops it was a foraging operation; to plantation residents, it was the Armageddon-like end of an era.)

Abraham Lincoln, Second Inaugural Address, March 4, 1865:

With malice toward none; with charity for all; with firmness in the right, as God gives us to see the right, let us strive on to finish the work we are in; to bind up the nation's wounds; to care for him who shall have borne the battle, and for his widow, and his orphan—to do all which may achieve and cherish a just, and a lasting peace, among ourselves, and with all nations.

. . . **March 4.** Lincoln reinaugurated; second inaugural address blames war on slavery, proposes charity for enemies . . . .

Mary A. Dodge to Abraham Lincoln, March 4, 1865,
Hamilton, Massachusetts:

I only wish to thank you for being so good—and to say
how sorry we all are that you must have four years more
of this terrible toil. But remember what a triumph it is
for the right, what a blessing to the country—and then
your rest shall be glorious when it does come!

(Lincoln was reinaugurated President of the United States on
the day this letter was written.)

Gen. William T. Sherman, recalling his last conference with
Lincoln, aboard the *River Queen,* City Point, Virginia, March
27, 1865:

Both General Grant and myself supposed that one or
the other of us would have to fight one more bloody
battle, and that it would be the *last.* Mr. Lincoln ex-
claimed, more than once, that there had been blood
enough shed, and asked us if another battle could not be
avoided. I remember well to have said that we could not
control that event; that this necessarily rested with our
enemy; and I inferred that both Jeff. Davis and General
Lee would be forced to fight one more desperate and
bloody battle. . . .

He [Lincoln] said . . . all he wanted of us was to defeat
the opposing armies, and to get the men composing the
Confederate armies back to their homes, at work on
their farms and in their shops. As to Jeff. Davis, he was
hardly at liberty to speak his mind fully, but intimated

that he ought to clear out, "escape the country," only it would not do for him to say so openly. As usual, he illustrated his meaning by a story: "A man once had taken the total-abstinence pledge. When visiting a friend, he was invited to take a drink, but declined, on the score of his pledge; when his friend suggested lemonade, which was accepted. In preparing the lemonade, the friend pointed to the brandy-bottle, and said the lemonade would be more palatable if he were to pour in a little brandy; when his guest said, if he could do so 'unbeknown' to him, he would not object." From which illustration I inferred that Mr. Lincoln wanted Davis to escape, "unbeknown" to him.

Brig. Gen. Joshua Lawrence Chamberlain, recalling the casualties of the battles at Quaker Road and White Oak Road, Virginia, March 29 and 31, 1865:

We had with us, to keep and to care for, more than five hundred bruised bodies of men—men made in the image of God, marred by the hand of man, and must we say in the name of God? And where is the reckoning for such things? And who is answerable? One might almost shrink from the sound of his own voice, which had launched into the palpitating air words of order . . . fraught with such ruin. Was it God's command we heard, or His forgiveness we must forever implore?

. . . **March 11.** Sherman captures Fayetteville, North Carolina . . . **March 19–21.** Union victory at Battle of Bentonville, North Carolina . . . **March 27.** Lincoln holds final council of war with Grant, Sherman, Porter, aboard *River Queen*, City Point, Virginia. . . . .

Sgt. Samuel Clear, 116th Pennsylvania Volunteer Infantry
(Irish Brigade), diary entry, March 31, 1865, Five Forks,
Virginia:

The woods was full of the ghastly Corpses of the dead,
and the shrieks of the wounded and dying mingled with
the crack of the musket and rumble of the artillery was
calculated to impress the whole upon the mind so indeli-
bly that it would last as long as life continued. As I was
running past a wounded rebel he caught me by the Pant
leg and held me so tight I had to beat his hand loose with
my gun. He wanted me to help him off the field.

Varina Howell Davis, recalling her departure from Richmond,
late March 1865:

With hearts bowed down by despair, we left Richmond. Mr. Davis almost gave way, when our little Jeff
begged him to remain with him, and Maggie clung to
him convulsively, for it was evident he thought he was
looking his last upon us.

(Jefferson Davis later joined his wife in exile after the Confederate government evacuated its capital city on April 2. They
were reunited, and seized together on May 10, 1865, at Ir-
winsville, Georgia. Davis died in 1889; Mrs. Davis lived until
1906.)

Phoebe Yates Pember, matron of Chimborazo Hospital, diary
entries, April 2, 1865, Richmond, Virginia:

The scene at the station was of indescribable confusion. No one could afford to abandon any article of wear
or household use, when going where they knew that
nothing could be replaced. Baggage was as valuable as
life, and life was represented there by wounded and sick
officers and men, helpless women and children, for all
who could be with the army were at their post. Hour
after hour fled and still the work went on. The streets
were strewn with torn papers, records and documents
too burdensome to carry away, too important to be left
for inspection, and people still thronged the thorough-
fares, loaded with stores until then hoarded by the government and sutler shops. The scream and rumble of
the cars never ceased all that weary night, and was perhaps the most painful sound to those left behind; for all
the rest of the city seemed flying. . . . No one slept during that night of horror, for added to the present scenes
were the anticipation of what the morrow would bring
forth. Daylight dawned upon a wreck of destruction and
devastation.

The Conquering Army Enters Richmond

They were well mounted, well accoutered, well fed—a
rare sight in Southern streets—the advance of that
vaunted army that for four years had so hopelessly

. . . **April 2.** Confederate government abandons Richmond, as capital falls to Union.

knocked at the gates of the Southern Confederacy. . . . Company after company, regiment after regiment, battalion after battalion, and brigade after brigade, they poured into the doomed city—an endless stream . . . [marching] through fire and smoke, over burning fragments of buildings, emerging at times like a phantom army when the wind lifted the dark clouds; while the colored population shouted and cheered them on their way.

Sarah A. "Sallie" Putnam, remembering the fall of Richmond, April 2, 1865:

In the alarm . . . the guards of the State Penitentiary fled from their posts, and numbers of the lawless and desperate villains incarcerated there, for crimes of every grade and hue, after setting fire to the workshops, made good the opportunity for escape; and, donning garments stolen wherever they could get them, in exchange for their prison livery, roamed over the city like fierce, ferocious beasts. . . . Into every house terror penetrated.

Private Carlton McCarthy, Richmond Howitzers, Cutshaw's Battalion Artillery, ca. April 3, 1865, between Petersburg and Richmond, Virginia:

To be one day without anything to eat was common. Two day's fasting, marching and fighting was not uncommon, and there were times when no rations were issued for three or four days. On one march, from Petersburg to Appomattox, no rations were issued to Cut-shaw's battalion of artillery for one entire week, and the men subsisted on the corn intended for the battery horses, raw bacon captured from the enemy, and the water of springs, creeks, and rivers.

Hailing—and Damning—the Conquering Hero

Forty or fifty freedmen—sole possessors of themselves for twenty-four hours—were at work on the bank of the canal, under the direction of a lieutenant, securing some floating timber. They crowded around the President, forgetting work in their wild joy at beholding the face of the author of the great Emancipation Proclamation. As he approached, I said to a colored woman, "There is the man who made you free." "What, massa?" "That is President Lincoln." "Dat President Linkum?" "Yes." She gazed at him a moment in amazement, joy, rapture, as if in supernal presence, then clapped her hands, jumped and shouted, "Glory! Glory! Glory!"

—Charles Carleton Coffin, reporting Lincoln's visit to conquered Richmond, April 4, 1865

("This must have been President Davis' chair," a tired Lincoln said when he first sat down inside the abandoned Confederate executive mansion after walking the streets of Richmond to a triumphant, emotional greeting by the city's newly liber-

. . . **April 3.** Grant captures Petersburg, Virginia . . . **April 4.** Lincoln visits Richmond.

ated black population. But most of Richmond's white citizens did not share their ex-slaves' enthusiasm.)

Our President's house! Ah, it is a bitter pill! I would that dear old house, with all its associations so sacred to Southerners, so sweet to us as a family, had shared in the general conflagration. Then its history would have been unsullied, though sad. Oh, how gladly would I have seen it burn!

> —*Judith W. McGuire, writing in her* Diary of a Southern Refugee During the War, *after the "violation" of Lincoln's visit to Richmond, April 4, 1865*

Varina Howell Davis to Mary Boykin Chesnut, April 7, 1865, Charlotte, North Carolina:

After life's fitful fever is o'er, I sleep well. Out of the depths of wretchedness and uncertainty, the *worst* has raised and buoyed me a little. I, at least, expect nothing more just now of a public nature. Like Shanks Evans's legs, "the conformation of the recruit won't admit of any more." So I am sitting down, taking account of my dead hopes. There is one effect of this stifling pressure upon us which is not altogether undesirable—we are benumbed.

. . . **April 7.** Grant urges Lee to surrender Army of Northern Virginia. . . . .

Gen. Ulysses S. Grant to Gen. Robert E. Lee, April 7, 1865:

The results of the last week must convince you of the hopelessness of further resistance on the part of the Army of Northern Virginia in this struggle. I feel that it is so, and regard it as my duty to shift from myself the responsibility of any further effusion of blood, by asking of you the surrender of that portion of the Confederate Southern Army known as the Army of Northern Virginia.

(Lee replied by asking Grant's terms; two days later, he surrendered at Appomattox Court House with these words: "I ask a suspension of hostilities pending the adjustment of the terms of surrender of this army, in the interview requested in my former communication today.")

Gen. Ulysses S. Grant, recalling the surrender scene inside the McLean house, Appomattox Court House, Virginia, April 9, 1865:

General Lee was dressed in a full uniform which was entirely new, and was wearing a sword of considerable value. . . . In my rough traveling suit, the uniform of a private with the straps of a lieutenant-general, I must have contrasted very strangely with a man so handsomely dressed. . . . What General Lee's feelings were I do not know. As he was a man of much dignity, with an impassible face, it was impossible to say whether he felt inwardly glad that the end had finally come, or felt sad over the result, and was too manly to show it. Whatever his feelings, they were entirely concealed from my observation; but my own feelings, which had been quite jubilant on the receipt of his letter, were sad and depressed. I felt like anything rather than rejoicing at the downfall of a foe who had fought so long and valiantly, and had suffered so much for a cause, though that cause was, I believe, one of the worst for which a people ever fought, and one for which there was the least excuse.

Sylvanus Cadwallader, New York *Herald,* describing Lee at the surrender scene at Appomattox, April 9, 1865:

During the whole interview he was retired and dignified to a degree bordering on taciturnity, but was free from all exhibition of temper or mortification. His demeanor was that of a thoroughly possessed gentleman who had a very disagreeable duty to perform, but was determined to get through it as well and as soon as he could.

Gen. Horace Potter, attached to Gen. Grant's staff, at Appomattox Court House, Virginia, April 9, 1865:

Lee signaled to his orderly to bring up his horse, and while the animal was being bridled the general stood on the lowest step, and gazed sadly in the direction of the valley beyond, where his army lay—now an army of prisoners. He thrice smote the palm of his left hand slowly with his right fist in an absent sort of way, seemed not to see the group of Union officers in the yard, who rose respectfully at his approach, and seemed unaware of everything about him. . . . The approach of his horse seemed to recall him, from his reverie, and he at once mounted. General Grant now stepped down from the porch, moving toward him, and saluted him by raising his hat. He was followed in this act of courtesy by all our officers present. Lee raised his hat respectfully, and rode off at a slow trot to break the sad news to the brave fellows whom he had so long commanded.

(As one of Lee's field commanders echoed in a postwar memoir: "What man could have laid down his sword at the feet of a victorious general with greater dignity?")

William Miller Owen, Confederate Officer, describing Gen. Robert E. Lee's return to his army after surrendering to Gen. Grant, April 9, 1865:

Whole lines of men rushed down to the roadside and crowded around him to shake his hand. All tried to show him the veneration and esteem in which they held him. Filled with emotion, he essayed to speak, but could only say, "Men, we have fought through the war together. I have done the best that I could for you. My heart is too full to say more." We all knew the pathos of those simple words, of that slight tremble in his voice, and it was no shame on our manhood "that something upon the soldier's cheek washed off the stains of powder"; that our tears answered to those in the eyes of our grand old chieftain; and that we could grasp the hand of "Uncle Robert" and pray *"God help you, General!"*

The Army of the Potomac Victorious

Mad hurrahs fill the air like the rolling of thunder, in the fields, in the woods, along the roads. . . . Caps fly in the air; the colors are waved in salute . . . the musicians fill the air with the joyous notes of "Yankee Doodle" and the sonorous strains of "Hail Columbia". . . . All the hopes of four years at last realized; all the fears dissipated, all perils disappeared; all the privations, all the sufferings, all the misery ended; the intoxication of triumph; the joy of the near return to the domestic hearth—for all this, one single burst of enthusiasm did not suffice. So the hurrahs and cries of joy were prolonged.

> —Gen. Regis de Trobriand reporting the reaction of
> Union troops to the news of General Lee's surrender,
> April 9, 1865

William Swinton, the New York *Times,* recalling the "mutual helpfulness" that pervaded both armies after Lee's surrender, April 9, 1865:

If the one army drank the joy of victory and the other the bitter draught of defeat, it was a joy moderated by the recollection of the cost at which it had been purchased, and a defeat mollified by the consciousness of many triumphs. If the victors could recall a Malvern Hill, an Antietam, a Gettysburg, a Five Forks, the vanquished could recall a Manassas, a Fredericksburg, a Chancellorsville, a Cold Harbor. How terrible had been the struggle!

Maj. Edward M. Boykin of South Carolina, remembering how the news of Lee's surrender was received by Confederate troops, April 9, 1865, near Appomattox Court House, Virginia:

[Soldiers came] to their officers with tears streaming from their eyes, and asked what it all meant, and would, at that moment, I know, have rather died the night before than see the sun rise on such a day as this.

Henry Kyd Douglas on the surrender of Confederate arms at Appomattox, April 12, 1865:

When the time came to march out and give up our guns and flags, in surrender . . . [my brigade was] the last to stack arms. . . . As my decimated and ragged band with their bullet-torn banner marched to its place, someone in the blue line broke the silence and called for three cheers for the last brigade to surrender. It was taken up all about him by those who knew what it meant. But for us this soldierly generosity was more than we could bear. Many of the grizzled veterans wept like women, and my own eyes were as blind as my voice was dumb. Years have passed since then and time mellows memories, and now I almost forget the keen agony of that bitter day when I recall how that line of blue broke its respectful silence to pay such tribute, at Appomattox, to the little line in grey that had fought them to the finish and only surrendered because it was destroyed.

Brig. Gen. Joshua Lawrence Chamberlain, accepting the formal surrender of the Army of Northern Virginia, Appomattox Court House, Virginia, April 12, 1865:

On our part not a sound of trumpet more, nor roll of drum; not a cheer, nor word nor whisper of vain-glorying, nor motion of man standing again at the order, but an awed stillness rather, and breath-holding, as if it were the passing of the dead!

. . .

Pvt. Carlton McCarthy, Richmond Howitzers, Cutshaw's Battalion Artillery, April 12, 1865, camp near Appomattox, Virginia:

Early in the morning . . . without the stirring drum or the bugle call of old, the camp awoke to the new life. Whether or not they had a country these soldiers did not know. Home to many, when they reached it, was graves and ashes. At any rate, there must be, somewhere on earth, a better place than a muddy, smoky camp in a

. . . **April 12.** Army of Northern Virginia stacks arms at Appomattox. . . . .

piece of scrubby pines—better company than gloomy, hungry comrades and inquisitive enemies, and something in the future more exciting, if not more hopeful, than nothing to eat, nowhere to sleep, nothing to do, and nowhere to go.

Rev. Henry Ward Beecher, oration at the rededication of Fort Sumter, Charleston, South Carolina, April 14, 1865:

On this solemn and joyful day we again lift to the breeze our father's flag, now again the banner of the United States, with the fervent prayer that God would crown it with honor, protect it from treason, and send it down to our children with all the blessings of civilization, liberty, and religion. Terrible in battle, may it be beneficent in peace. Happily no bird or beast of prey has been inscribed upon it. The stars that redeem the night from darkness, and the beams of red light that beautify the morning, have been united upon its folds. As long as the sun endures, or the stars, may it wave over a nation neither enslaved nor enslaving.

At Lincoln's Deathbed

The giant sufferer lay extended diagonally across the bed, which was not long enough for him. He had been stripped of his clothes. His large arms, which were occasionally exposed, were of a size which one would scarce

. . . **April 14.** Lincoln shot at Ford's Theatre by actor John Wilkes Booth; Secretary of State William H. Seward attacked by Booth accomplice. . . . .

have expected from his spare appearance. His slow, full respiration lifted the clothes with each breath he took. His features were calm and striking. I had never seen them appear to better advantage.

> —*Secretary of the Navy Gideon Welles, diary entry,*
> *April 15, 1865, Washington*

Death of a President

Now he belongs to the ages.

> —*Secretary of War Edwin M. Stanton, words at Lincoln's*
> *deathbed, April 15, 1865, Washington*

I cried and cried that day, and for days I was so depressed I could scarcely force myself to work.

> —*Samuel Gompers, factory boy and future labor leader,*
> *remembering his reaction to Lincoln's death,*
> *April 15, 1865*

Hurrah! Old Abe Lincoln is dead!

> —*South Carolina girl, on hearing news of Lincoln's death,*
> *April 15, 1865*

A while ago, Lincoln's chief occupation was thinking what death, thousands who ruled like lords when he was

. . . **April 15.** Lincoln dies. . . . .

cutting logs, should die. A moment more, and the man who was progressing to murder countless human beings, is interrupted in his work by the shot of an assassin. . . . Where does patriotism end, and murder begin? And considering that every one is closely watched, and that five men have been killed this day for expressing their indifference on the death of Mr. Lincoln, it would be best to postpone this discussion.

—*Sarah Morgan, diary entry on the death of Lincoln,*
April 15, 1865, Baton Rouge, Louisiana

Rev. Henry Lyman Morehouse of the First Baptist Church, East Saginaw, Michigan, remembering how the news of Lincoln's murder first reached his community, April 15, 1865:

Business stopped; hearts throbbed almost audibly; knots of men congregated on the streets; telegraph offices were thronged by anxious faces; and all were incredulous that such a stupendous, nefarious transaction had occurred in America. . . . Laughter ceased. Trembling lips, tearful eyes, saddened countenances, and suppressed tones evinced the unspeakable emotions of the soul. The heart of the nation had been pierced and every member became numb. . . . America mourns as she has never mourned before.

Pvt. William A. Hamblin, 4th Massachusetts Heavy Artillery, to his wife, April 16, 1865, from Fort Barnard:

I suppose you have all heard the dreadful news of the murder of the President ere this. It does not seem possible that he could have been killed in the manner he was, after having for the last four years passed through so much danger with his life in his hand, to be at last struck down by a drunken, miserable play actor, a dissipated fool who did not know when he had done the deed and cried "Revenge for the South" that he had killed a man who had that day been kindly urging the mild treatment of the rebels and who has on more occasions than one risked his reputation for honesty of purpose to shield the South from the just desserts that she was receiving and has always stood ready to listen to any decent proposals for terminating the war. In killing the President the South has lost their *best* friend.

Sgt. Samuel Clear, 116th Pennsylvania Volunteer Infantry (Irish Brigade), diary entry, April 17, 1865, Berksville Station, Virginia:

A silent gloom fell upon us like a pall. No one spoke or moved, our sorrow was so great that we could scarcely realize what had happened. I always thought that he [Lincoln] was the most loved by all the Army and people of America, but I am now sure of that. The "Stars and Stripes" was quietly lowered, and old torn shreds of Flags almost slipped out of the hands of the Color Sargeants. The Regiments was quietly dismissed and we moved away slowly to our quarters, as if we each had lost a near and dear friend at home. Quietly, quietly we went to our rest. Was anybody glad, if he was he made no sign, and well for them they did not, for they never would have reached home alive. No drill, No Dress Parade. No Nothing all quiet, Flags at half mast, lonesome was no words for us. It was like going from a busy City to a fastness in the mountains, what a hold Old Honest Abe Lincoln had on the hearts of the soldiers.

Mary Boykin Chesnut, diary entry, April 22, 1865, Chester, South Carolina:

Lincoln—old Abe Lincoln—killed—murdered— Seward wounded! Why? By whom? It is simply maddening, all of this. . . . I know this foul murder will bring down worse miseries on us. Mary Darby says: "But they murdered him themselves. No Confederates in Washington." "But if they see fit to accuse us of investigating it?" "Who murdered him?" "Who knows!" "See if they don't take vengeance on us, now that we are ruined and cannot repel them any longer." Met Mr. Heyward. He said . . . the death of Lincoln—I call that a warning to tyrants. He will not be the last president put to death in the capital, though he is the first."

Another Surrender

General [Joseph] Johnston and I entered the small frame-house. We asked the farmer if we could have the use of his house for a few minutes, and he and his wife withdrew into a smaller log-house, which stood close by.

As soon as we were alone together, I showed him the dispatch announcing Mr. Lincoln's assassination, and watched him closely. The perspiration came out in large drops in his forehead, and he did not attempt to conceal his distress. He denounced the act as a disgrace to the age, and hoped I did not charge it to the Confederate Government. I told him I could not believe that he or General Lee, or the officers of the Confederate army, could possibly be privy to acts of assassination; but I would not say as much for Jeff. Davis.

> —Gen. William T. Sherman, recalling the surrender of
> Johnston's army at the Bennett House, near Greensboro,
> North Carolina, April 26, 1865

How Yankees and Rebels Waged Peace

I found that the farm work my father was then engaged in was cutting and shucking corn. So, the morning after my arrival, I doffed my uniform of first lieutenant, put on some of my father's old clothes and proceeded to wage war on the standing corn.

> —Lt. Leander Stilwell, 100th Indiana Volunteers, on his
> arrival home, ca. June 1865

Were these things real? Did I see those brave and noble countrymen of mine laid low in death and welter-

. . . **April 26.** Johnston surrenders to Sherman at Greensboro, North Carolina . . . **May 10.** Davis captured by Union troops, wearing wife's raglan in futile effort to disguise himself . . . **May 22.** Davis imprisoned at Fort Monroe, Virginia . . . .

ing in their blood? Did I see our country laid waste and in ruins . . . smoldering cities and deserted homes? Did I see the flag of my country, that I had followed so long, furled to be no more unfurled forever? Surely they are the vagaries of mine own imagination. . . . But, hush! I now hear the approach of battle. That low, rumbling sound in the West is the roar of cannon in the distance.

—*Pvt. Samuel Watkins, 1st Tennessee Regiment, C.S.A.,*
after returning home, ca. June 1865

Edmund Ruffin, diary entry, June 17, 1865, from "Malbourne," his estate near Richmond, Virginia:

I hereby declare my unmitigated hatred to Yankee rule—to all political, social & business connection with Yankees—and to the Yankee race. Would that I could impress these sentiments, in their full force, on every living Southerner, & bequeath them to everyone yet to be born! May such sentiments be held universally in the outraged & down-trodden South, although in silence & stillness, until the now far-distant day shall arrive for just retribution for Yankee usurpation, oppression, & atrocious outrages—& for deliverance & vengeance for the now ruined, subjugated, & enslaved Southern States! . . . I hereby repeat . . . my unmitigated hatred . . . to the perfidious, malignant, & vile Yankee race.

(After writing this entry in his diary, the man who had fired the first shot of the Civil War placed the barrel of his rifle in his

... **June 17.** Edmund Ruffin commits suicide near Richmond, Virginia ....

mouth and depressed the trigger with a stick, killing himself instantly.)

Neither slavery nor involuntary servitude, except as a punishment for crime whereof the party shall have been duly convicted, shall exist within the United States, or any place subject to their jurisdiction. Congress shall have power to enforce this article by appropriate legislation.

—Thirteenth Amendment to the Constitution of the United States, abolishing slavery, ratified December 18, 1865

... **December 18.** The Thirteenth Amendment to the Constitution is ratified, and slavery is finally destroyed forever . . . .

WITNESS TO WAR SERIES

__*WITNESS TO WAR: KOREA* by Rod Paschall
0-399-51934-3/$12.00
From the post–World War II division to the first Soviet-American political tensions, the June 1950 invasion to the truce talks, *Witness to War: Korea* is the story of the war in the words of those who fought it. Includes seven maps, twenty never-before-published photographs, and a running timeline of events.

__*WITNESS TO WAR: VIETNAM* by Maurice Isserman
0-399-52162-3/$12.00
The most controversial war in United States history comes alive through the words of the people who lived it—soldiers and civilians, officers and political leaders, reporters and diplomats. From the anticolonial uprisings in the 1940s to the crushing defeat of South Vietnam in 1975, this book provides a perspective that goes beyond the battlefields—to offer new insight into events that shaped the course of American history.

__*WITNESS TO WAR: THE CIVIL WAR 1861–1865*
edited by Harold Holzer 0-399-52203-4/$12.50
The letters, speeches and anecdotes of both Union and Confederate soldiers—some in print for the first time—give a broad and wide-ranging vision of the terrifying battles waged. Featuring writings from leaders such as Abraham Lincoln, Jefferson Davis and Robert E. Lee, as well as letters sent home from brave front-line soldiers, these narratives provide a stunning true-to-life portrait of the Civil War.

MILITARY REFERENCE

__The Army Times Book of Great Land Battles: From
the Civil War to the Gulf War
by Colonel J. D. Morelock; edited by Walter J. Boyne
                                    0-425-14371-6/$29.95
*A fascinating, in-depth look at fourteen of the most important
land battles in military history.*

__Encyclopedia of Modern U.S. Military Weapons
by Colonel Timothy M. Laur and Steven L. Llanso
                                    0-425-14781-9/$39.95
*A comprehensive and complete reference of the principal
weapons systems of the United States.*

__Generals in Muddy Boots: A Concise Encyclopedia
of Combat Commanders
*by Dan Cragg, Sergeant Major, U.S. Army (retired),
edited by Walter J. Boyne*   0-425-15136-0/$29.95
*The dramatic true life stories of the 300 most courageous and
skilled combat commanders throughout history, from Alexander
the Great to Joan of Arc. (A collaboration with the Army Times)*

__Clash of Chariots: The Great Tank Battles
by Tom Donnelly and Sean Naylor, edited by Walter J. Boyne
                                    0-425-15307-X/$31.95
*This incisive work outlines the tactics and operations employed
in the major tank campaigns of the twentieth century, from
Germany's 1940 blitzkreig to the 1991 Gulf War.*